MORE DORY'S STORIES

D.J. DeSai

iUniverse, Inc.
Bloomington

More Dory's Stories

iUniverse books may be ordered through booksellers or by contacting:

iUniverse
1663 Liberty Drive
Bloomington, IN 47403
www.iuniverse.com
1-800-Authors (1-800-288-4677)

ISBN: 978-1-4502-6568-3 (pbk)
ISBN: 978-1-4502-6567-6 (cloth)
ISBN: 978-1-4502-6566-9 (ebk)

Library of Congress Control Number: 2010915436

Printed in the United States of America

iUniverse rev. date: 11/22/10

CONTENTS

INTRODUCTION

Life is full of adventure and opportunities for personal and spiritual growth, and this seems especially true for Dory and her loved ones. Whether on vacation, in or out of town, or just at home, they all have encountered many remarkable and entertaining situations from which they have drawn important lessons. Some of these lessons were hard-learned, some unpleasant, and others just fun. *More Dory's Stories* is part of a project of sharing these experiences for the pleasure and benefit of readers, so that they might take these important morals into their own hearts and souls.

Hopefully you will see this collection as a meaningful reflection of your own life, and will find comfort and joy in seeing your own spirit on the page. Or maybe you will have the opportunity to hear of experiences much different from your own, and see the world through the mind and heart of Dory instead. At least—and at best, perhaps—you are sure to find, as Dory has, that these stories reveal God, and help us to appreciate the many and varied ways He challenges us, guides us, and speaks to us each day.

As many of you well know from *Dory's "Oh My God" Stories* (2009), Dory's energy and dedication to life and God are an inspiration to read. They represent a lifetime of lessons-learned, and deserve to be shared. And one volume just wasn't enough!

If you enjoy reading inspirational, as well as incredible, short stories that have actually taken place in real life, you will find great pleasure in this brilliantly-written book consisting of thirty-three nonfiction events that will send your imagination and emotions soaring to an all-time high. Each magnificent journey or extreme predicament will surely attract any reader to every story and each line of poetry by D.J. DeSai.

The author feels the need to inform the reader that each *"Oh my God!"* phrase in every story *is certainly not used as slang*. The stanzas are actually written as prayers to God.

IN HONOR OF

My mother, Lois Sea.
I am proud to put the words "Mom, I love you with all my heart" in writing. You are more than wonderful. You are an angel. Thank you for everything!

My dad, the late James Sea, my brother, the late Jimmy Sea, my aunt, the late Helen Hayes, my children, Missy and Jeff, my brothers, Tommy and Danny, all my family, friends, co-workers, and clients.

Thanks for the support. May God bless and keep each one of you safe. I love you all!

SPECIAL MENTION OF

Our God and Savior, Jesus Christ.

The late, great Tim Crabtree, for helping me to gain a better understanding of God's precious mercy, forgiveness, and love.

The late, great musician and singer songwriter Tim Krekel, for his encouragement, and whose artistry filled my heart with only peace, love, and dance.

My high school English teacher, Judy Pollard, who inspired me to always write.

All of my loved ones, including my editors, Vickie Cochran and Nellgato Lueck.

Demolition Derby Race

A surprise can be described as happy or sad,
It can also leave us feeling glad or mad.

D.J. DeSai

Have you ever known a person who is very adventurous, and seemingly afraid of nothing? I have, and this special man is my daddy. Even though he passed away several years ago, I will always have many reasons to think of him. He was so amazing. I define him as being "one of a kind," and there is not one single day that passes by when I don't feel a great love for him. However, there have been times when I did not always agree with his decisions and actions, although I tried to understand them. This story is a perfect example of what I am referring to.

One sultry summer day, around four o'clock in the afternoon, I sat on the front porch of my parents' home with nothing much to do. It was too hot to play any of the games that my friends and I enjoyed participating in outdoors, so I was very excited when my daddy staggered up the sidewalk and asked the entire family if we wanted to go out and have a little fun that night. He had a smile on his face and a daring look in his eyes that told me he was all but sober from the alcohol I knew he had been drinking. I screamed out, "Yes!" with joy in my voice. He looked at me and laughed. Then he said, "Go get ready, Dory." After being so bored, I couldn't wait to leave the house.

My daddy, Amos, didn't mind taking us to the car races, horse races, and music events. These three hobbies were what he loved the most, and I was just thrilled that he was in the mood to go somewhere that night. Anywhere was fine with me.

Ever since I can remember, the rest of my family, including myself, had grown fond of all my dad's interests. Of course, he loved the car races because he built and raced his own cars; he loved the horse races because he owned a few of them; and he loved music because he was an excellent guitar player. He also had his own band, and the band members loved playing in the nightclubs, for private parties, and at family reunions.

Leola, my mother, started getting ready. I could tell she was very excited about getting to go out somewhere because I could see a glow all over her face. She worked very hard every day of the week, so she deserved some time out. We were all entitled to some fun together.

Around seven o'clock that night, we piled into our beautiful, four-door Dodge and took off down the road. I loved that car so much. It was a pretty candy apple red color, and it did not have a scratch on it. It was also the newest and shiniest looking car my dad had ever owned, although I had overheard him complaining about several mechanical problems he had been having with it. No matter; I felt very proud to be riding in it.

My dad drove a few blocks down the road before he turned into the Motor Speedway's parking lot entrance. This told me without a doubt that we were headed for the car races again, but that was okay. I just wanted to get out of the house and do something; I didn't care what it was. After we arrived inside the gates and had sat down, I heard the announcer speaking. I heard him say that it was Demolition Derby night, and the races were scheduled to start at eight o'clock. I was sure a lot of fun was headed our way, just as my dad had suggested earlier that afternoon. Demolition Derby races were always very thrilling. During this event, each driver gets to test his car wrecking skill by putting the pedal to the metal while crashing into all the other cars. The last car left running is the one declared the winner of the race. Actually, I was fonder of this type of race than the drag racing my dad usually participated in. There was seldom a dull moment watching all the cars get smashed up, while drag racing seemed a little less exciting.

Dad gave Mom some money so she could buy some popcorn and drinks, and then he told her that he would be back shortly. His leaving the family during the races didn't surprise me much. He liked socializing with the other race car drivers and pit stop workers. He knew most of them fairly well from being involved with the sport himself.

A few minutes later, I looked out on the track. *Oh, wow!* I thought. I was very startled. Directly in the midst of all the banged up and beat up looking demolition derby cars sat our nice-looking family car. I wondered why in the world our car was sitting out there with all the others. It really stood out among the race cars because it was such a newer model with no exotic paint or number on it, nor had it been wrecked numerous times before. At first I wondered if my dad were going to drive someone else's car in the race. I watched every move on the track as my heart thumped with excitement and fear. Soon, I saw my dad get into our family car at the same time all the other drivers got into their own. Then I heard the announcer speaking through the microphone, saying it was time for the drivers to start their engines.

"Oh my God," I whispered to Jesus. I could not believe my eyes. I wondered what my dad was thinking and what in the world he was doing out there on the track with our car. It didn't take very long for me to figure it out. Soon, he started ramming our shiny red car into every other car that got in his way. The other drivers were doing the same thing. I said a silent prayer while I sat there and watched in disbelief as our beautiful family vehicle quickly turned into a crushed up, piece-of-nothing-but-junk car in just a matter of a few minutes. Our car started smoking all over the place. Both sides of all four doors, the front bumper and grill, and the rear end of it were either completely dented in or ripped to pieces. I could see different parts of the car flying in the air or lying on the race track where they had just fallen off after being pushed around and rammed into so badly. I knew our four-door Dodge was living its last few seconds, and I still could not believe what I was seeing. Finally, it was over. The car could not or would not move anymore. It was definitely dead.

I looked up at my mom sitting there with her mouth wide open and a pale look on her face. *She appears very faint,* I thought to myself. *Is she sick? Will she pass out? Is she so mad she can't see straight?* I wondered. I thought I knew how my mom felt, but I wasn't sure. I was thinking that maybe everyone else was all having trouble believing what they had just seen, too, because I certainly was. Not only was our car a lost mess, but the whole family seemed to be, too. I was sure they all felt the same numb and sick feelings as I did.

Fun? I asked myself, as I kept remembering my dad asking us if we were ready to go have some fun earlier that afternoon. I was not sure the word "fun" was the most appropriate word he could have used, because it sure didn't look

like Mom was having too much fun. It hadn't seemed like a very good time for any of us, for that matter. I couldn't help but wonder how entertaining it had been for my daddy.

The entire family, including my dad, had to be driven home that night by my aunt and uncle who happened to be there, too. I will never forget the silence in the car that night on our way home. You could have heard a pin drop. I was sure everyone, counting my dad, was thinking about the previously pretty red family car. Yes, it was completely totaled. I was also certain that no one, including the junk yard owner, would have wanted the car after that race. I still could not believe what my dear dad had done. I was sure I knew why, though.

Everyone, as well as myself, knew that Dad had been very upset in the past concerning the family car. He had tried to fix a certain problem more than a few times, but had no luck. No one else could repair it either, and he had spent a lot of money on it. I had heard him raise his frustrated voice numerous times concerning the car on a few other occasions. It had aggravated him tremendously, so I guessed he wanted revenge, or maybe he just needed to vent. Totaling the car could have been a stress release for my dad. I had also overheard him tell his buddies that he felt like running the car off in a ditch somewhere. I heard him say that the vehicle was not worth a dime. I couldn't help but think that our car would have been worth a lot more before then than what it was now. It didn't matter much, though. It was gone. Destroyed!

The next day Dad went out and bought another car. He drove it home, and no one ever talked about that Demolition Derby night again. I have often wondered, though, if he ever regretted demolishing the family car in a race that he never even won. I hoped and prayed he had. I have to give him credit for one thing though: he's the only person I have ever known to follow through with something like this. Most people only talk about it, but never actually do it. No matter what, though, I tell myself that he was sorry for it because one thing is for sure. That was the last time he ever put the family car in a **"Demolition Derby race."**

The Sound of Death

*Listening close to every sound
Can sometimes hurt and bring us down.*

D.J. DeSai

I know for a fact that it's a good idea to listen more, versus always talking. I also know that sometimes listening can get us into trouble, especially if we're not supposed to be doing it. This story tells about a very personal experience that took place in my life and has proven this certain point to me.

Around the age of eight years old, my family and I moved from a pure country farm life to a small nearby town. My grandparents still lived in the country where they owned farms, and I missed them very much. When they came to visit, I would occasionally get to go back home with them and stay overnight. Sometimes I would stay for the entire weekend. It was nice being able to visit with both sets of grandparents and take turns going home with them. This enabled me still to enjoy the sweet taste of country life, and also to see and talk to my previous friends who lived nearby.

After my parents moved from the country, I found myself sitting around reliving memories of my past. I longed to hear the rooster's crow in the wee hours of the mornings, and I couldn't forget the times I gathered eggs for breakfast with my grandmother. I also had fond memories of riding the horses and running wild down by the old barn. I loved climbing on the haylofts too, and watching my grandfather care for the animals and the farmland. My grandparents were always busy doing chores, but they still managed to keep their eye on me.

One afternoon my mom's parents visited with us. Before they left, they told me it was their turn to take me home with them since I was out of school for summer break. They also told me that I was welcome to stay the entire week if I wanted to. I couldn't remember which grandparents I had stayed with the last time, but I was always happy and eager to go home with either of them. I was so thrilled when my mom said it was okay for me to go. "Oh, thank you!" I shouted. I couldn't wait to get back to the farm and also to see my school friends.

After a couple of days of running wild on the land, I became a little lonely and bored. It was smoldering hot outside, and I wanted someone my own age to spend time with. Later one afternoon, I found myself inside the house trying to stay cool. I wasn't really tired enough for a nap, so I sat there on the sofa trying to think of something to do. My grandmother was busy with chores, so I didn't want to bother her.

While looking around in every room for something to pass my time, I ended up staring at the telephone. Back in those days, most people who lived in that part of the country had a telephone service which included two or more households sharing the same phone line. They called their phone service a party line. A one-ring sequence of the phone was my grandparents' ring. Two rings belonged to their neighbors who lived one mile down the road and I wasn't sure who had the three-ring series. That ring was probably for someone who lived within a two or three mile radius of my grandparents' home.

It didn't take me long to pick up the telephone. I decided to call my other grandfather, who was my dad's dad. I missed him, too. My plan was to talk with him for a few minutes, and then I would call one of my classmates. As soon as I put the receiver to my ear, I heard two female voices talking to each other on the other two party lines that my grandparents shared. I immediately hung the phone up. I sat there for a couple of more minutes before picking it back up. Still, the two women were talking a mile a minute. I hung the phone back up again. Thinking the two of them may be on the phone for awhile, I decided to lie down and take a nap.

After a few minutes of lying there with my eyes closed, I knew I couldn't sleep. I picked up the phone for the third time. Again, the two busy bodies were still talking. I almost hung the phone up once more, but I didn't. I decided it would be fun to listen to what the other two parties were saying. I knew it was wrong to eavesdrop, but there was nothing else left to do. I was so restless. *Besides, they're hogging the phone line,* I told myself. *I can't call my grandfather or my friend because of them, so maybe if I stay on the phone, they will take the hint that I want to use it and hang up.*

While listening quietly to the two women talking about a man who had just been killed on a John Deere tractor that same morning, I couldn't believe what I was hearing. Evidently, the tractor had turned completely over on the man while he was turning it around on a hill. *Wow!* I thought to myself. *The poor man had lain out in the hot sun for most of that morning and part of the afternoon while the tractor had lain on top of his face and body before someone had found him. Gee!* I continued to listen closely to the two ladies as they described the gruesome way the man looked while lying there on the ground, buried by his own tractor. I heard them say they were not sure if he had died instantly or if he had suffered long. Both ladies said they hoped and prayed for the dead man's sake, that he had died instantly.

While sitting there feeling guilty listening to such a horrific story, and getting ready to hang up the phone, I overheard one of the women speak the name of the man who had been killed on the John Deere tractor. As I sat there in a total daze, my first thought was *I cannot believe what I just heard.* I also could not comprehend what I had just heard. I wanted to scream! *Oh my God,* I silently cried to Jesus, not wanting the two women to know I was listening to their conversation. *The dead man they must be referring to is my grandfather. He's my dad's dad. He's only forty years old and way too young to be dead,* I thought. *No, it can't be him! I was just with him a few days ago. I was just getting ready to call him on the telephone. I wonder if there could be another man with the same name as my grandfather. This thought is my only prayer,* I told myself.

Quickly and quietly, I hung the phone up as I sat there on the sofa in a child-like state of shock. Deep down inside, I knew it was my grandfather the two ladies were referring to. All I could do at that very moment was cry and reminisce about the times he had taken me for so many rides on that same John Deere tractor. Every time I would see him, he would pick me up and sit me up on his tractor. I would sit right there next to him, feeling very secure as we rode around enjoying the country view.

Each time my grandfather would take me back to the house and drop me off, he would pull a silver dollar out of his pocket and hand it to me before we said goodbye. I had saved each one of those silver dollars in a big glass jar. They were hidden under my bed for safe keeping. I was going to wait until I had enough of them saved up, and then I was going to buy myself a nice radio because I loved music so much. I couldn't wait to show my grandfather the radio I was going to buy with the coins. I wanted to let him listen to it too, while we were riding on his tractor.

Still, I could not believe my grandpa was really dead. He had to be though, because why else would the two women discuss such an awful event if it were not really true? *No, it has to be real,* I thought to myself, *as bad as it feels.*

While thinking about what to do next, I sat there and cried some more. I knew I needed to tell my grandmother so she could call my mom and dad and tell them. I wondered if my parents already knew. My poor dad would be so upset to find out that his dad had been killed by his own tractor turning over on him.

Feeling as though I wanted to die myself with my grandfather, I wasn't sure I really understood the total meaning of death. I was so young and naïve, being only eight years old. I also had never been to a funeral before. I wasn't really sure I could even endure it, or accept the concept of death at such a young age.

Still feeling the shock, I went into the kitchen and saw my grandmother, my mom's mom, sitting at the table peeling potatoes. I told her that I had eavesdropped on the party line telephone, telling her what I had overheard the two women say about my grandfather. My grandmother's eyes and mouth flew wide open. She was quick to tell me that if I were joking around, it was definitely not funny. I told her that it was not a joke. I told her that I was telling her the truth. She told me she was going to call my parents to ask them if it were really true. She asked me one last time if I wanted to change my story. I told her what I had heard again, so she picked up the phone and dialed my parents' phone number. *Gee! I wish I was there to console them because I know this will hurt them terribly,* I told myself.

I couldn't hear what was being said on my parents' end of the phone, but I heard my grandmother ask my mom if they had heard anything about anyone getting killed on a John Deere tractor. Then I heard my grandmother tell my mom she was so sorry that she had called and bothered them. I also heard her say that I was only a child and must have made the whole story up. I felt my heart sinking as I sat there feeling like a very bad girl. *Why had those two women made up a story like that?* I wondered. *I'm upset with myself for believing them.* After my very displeased grandmother got off the phone, she told me to go into the bedroom. She told me to stay there for as long as it took for me to say I was sorry about the lie I had told. She said it was wrong for me to make up such a tale and to worry everyone else with a story as terrible as that one.

Wow! I thought to myself. *It doesn't make sense to me. I did hate saying what I had said. I wish I could take it all back, but I had only told my grandmother exactly what I had overheard on the telephone, but no one had believed me. Oh well. I'm so glad the story is not true. The punishment is nothing compared to thinking and believing my grandfather is really dead,* I decided.

I was so tired after hearing and talking about the dreadful story. I lay down on the bed and went to sleep for a few minutes, and I dreamed about riding on the John Deere tractor with my grandfather again. I dreamed his tractor turned over on top of both of us but I was strong enough to push the heavy vehicle all the way off of us, so neither one of us had been hurt. Thank God, it was a good dream.

When I woke up, I went to the kitchen and apologized to my grandmother about the story I had told her. I decided I would not even bring it up again because I did not want to believe it either, and I chose not to think about it anymore myself. It was an upsetting thought, and it was so much better left alone.

A few minutes later the phone rang. It rang once before it paused so I knew it was my grandmother's ring. Immediately after she said hello, I knew something was wrong. "Oh my!" my grandmother gasped. It was my mom on the phone telling her that my story was true after all. My grandfather had been killed indeed on the John Deere tractor. He had lain in the sun for several hours with the tractor on top of him, just like the two women had said on the phone. I heard my grandmother tell my mom she was so sorry and that I could stay with her as long as she needed me to. I wasn't sure what else was said on the other end of the phone, but I was sure my parents were very saddened, and I was, too. I felt sick, hurt, and empty inside.

After they said their goodbyes, my grandmother walked over to me, and hugged me tight. Then she whispered in my ear and said, "Dory, I am so very sorry that I didn't believe you." She cried while telling me she was there for me if I needed her in any way, and that my grandfather was a very good man. She also said that he had gone to heaven to be with Jesus, and I would see him again someday. Then she hugged and kissed my face again to comfort me.

Feeling so distressed, I went to bed that night knowing I would not see my grandfather again in this life. I also knew I would never want to spend my silver dollars that he had given me. I would always keep them close by so I could look at them, feel them, and remember him giving them to me. I would miss him and the tractor rides so much, but if he were going to heaven, I knew he would be happy there. This made me happy too, even though I was not ready to lose him. I was hurting so badly inside and I couldn't help but wonder why God had taken him away from me. I was sure there was a good reason, though, and someday I would understand it.

Yes, this will truly be a day in my life that I will never forget. Even though I had to pay the consequences of how I learned of my grandfather's death, the entire ordeal had taught me something very important. I know without a doubt that I will never want to eavesdrop on the telephone again, not only because it is wrong, but also for fear of hearing **"the sound of death."**

Shoot and Kill Me

It may not be easy to follow your heart,
But always remember, it's one fine art.

D.J. DeSai

During my teenage years, I had a best friend named Jody. I can't forget the times that she and I often shared stories with each other regarding past events in our lives. Some of those tragic trials and tribulations seemed very devastating, so oftentimes it was very helpful for us to talk to each other about experiences that were still haunting our minds.

One day Jody cried hysterically while she revealed a very shocking and personal family incident to me. My friend recounted every atrocious moment and described each appalling detail to me regarding an occurrence that took place one night inside her home. I've decided to share her story because I truly believe it may help others, especially people who can relate.

Although Jody was given no choice but to go through this horrific ordeal, she would not trade it with anyone else on this earth. She truly believes that she actually had to live through this dilemma and many others to get to where she is today. Now, she thinks of herself as a happy, healthy, and thankful person. Some of those so-called happenings have allowed Jody to grow, so she is very grateful for them. "It's not a perfect world, but it's a content one most of the time," she says. "What more could a girl ask for?"

Jody knew her dad, Travis, had been out drinking alcohol on this one particular day. It was late when he finally walked in the back door, staggering all over the place. The sound of his arrival woke Jody up as usual, because after he'd been drinking he'd almost always come home fussing at whoever got in his way. That person was usually Jody's mom, Ruby.

Ruby could do no wrong in Jody's eyes. She went to work every day, came home, and took care of Jody and the rest of the family. She'd also get up every Sunday morning and take Jody and her siblings to church. She was a sweet woman and everyone who knew her felt the same way about her.

After Travis would get drunk and come home, oftentimes he'd wake Ruby and keep her up most of the night. He would argue with her about everything, but usually it was over nothing much. He'd look for anything to fuss about, and accuse Ruby of wrong doings though Jody knew her daddy's accusations were false. Ruby never had time to be a bad woman. It was only the alcohol talking inside of Travis. Nevertheless, Jody felt sorry for her mom, and resented her dad's ways. She still loved him, though.

Ruby loved Travis, too, despite the ways he treated her. She knew what was upsetting her husband. Travis had lost his parents at a very young age, so Ruby was sure the deaths were still eating at Travis's heart. The alcohol only numbed the pain he was still feeling.

Watching Travis walk through the door that night, Jody knew his behavior would not be any different than any other night after he'd been out drinking. The night would end on a sour note, as always. Her dad was drunk and ready to fight with her mom again. Jody wondered why he didn't pick on someone his own size. She hated the way he caused trouble at home with her mother, but she was so afraid of him, especially after he'd been drinking. Almost every bone in his body became mean, and Jody was afraid he would hurt her mom someday. She also knew he would be very sorry about it later if he did. *Maybe this is what it will take,* she thought, although she hoped and prayed her dad's anger would never get that out of hand.

That night Jody just lay there in bed as still as she could with her bedroom door barely open. She could see the light on in the living room, and her daddy sitting there yelling at her mother. Ruby was in the kitchen fixing Travis something to eat, and she wanted to go back to bed, but Travis kept cursing at her and calling her ugly names. Jody heard her mom tell her dad over and over to be quiet or he was going to wake up the kids. Travis didn't care. Jody remembered thinking she would never marry a man who acted that way and someday when she got older, she would whip her dad good for being so rude to her mom. *I'll teach him a lesson,* Jody thought. *Yes, he will be so sorry someday.*

Finally, Jody saw her dad get up off the couch and go into her parents' bedroom. She was hoping he was finally going to bed. About a minute later, Travis came out of the bedroom with something in his hand. As Jody laid there on her bed, she tried to see what he was carrying. Travis was turned around facing her mother so Jody couldn't tell what it was he had in his hand.

Casually, Ruby started to walk out of the kitchen. Suddenly, Jody heard her dad yell at her mom. He told her to walk over to where he was. Ruby said, "No, I'm going to bed now. Your food is ready; now go eat it." Jody heard her dad say, "I said get over here now or I'm going to use this gun on you!" as he pointed the gun directly at Ruby. Jody's heart started pounding extremely hard as she watched closely, feeling scared to death. Ruby walked over to where Travis was, just as he had told her to. He pressed on her head with the end of the gun as if he were going to pull the trigger and kill her. Jody thought her heart would stop beating. She was so horrified!

While she lay there paralyzed in her bed, she was unsure of what would happen next. "Oh my God!" Jody cried out to the Lord. "My dad is going to kill my mom. Help her Jesus!" Jody prayed. "She loves us, takes care of us, and we can't live without her. God, please! Don't let him shoot her."

Still lying there praying, all Jody could think about was her dad pulling the trigger of that gun and blowing her mom's head into a million pieces. If her dad killed her mom, it would kill everyone else, too. It would hurt them so badly. Jody still couldn't move a muscle. She was too scared! As she lay there in agony, she saw her dad shove the gun against her mother's head again, as if he needed to let her know he meant business. Then Jody heard her dad tell her mom he was going to shoot her. He said it with a voice that sounded as though he were truly going to do it. "Yes, he is going to kill her now!" Jody cried out to God. Her heart was racing out of control.

All of a sudden Jody heard herself scream as loudly as she possibly could. The sound of her own voice alarmed her. She couldn't believe the echo of the sharp, piercing, noise that had bellowed up from the bottom of her self. Anxiously, she covered her head underneath the bed covers. All she could think of that very moment was her dad shooting her mom and then turning the gun on her, his only daughter. Jody didn't care anymore.

She hoped her dad would shoot her instead of her mom. She knew her mother did not deserve this kind of treatment. Jody didn't think she deserved to die either, but she was ready to die for her mom. Not really sure of what might happen next, Jody just lay there as still as she possibly could. She was ready to take the bullets as she curled her tiny body up into a round ball, waiting for her own death to arrive.

Suddenly, there was nothing but a sweet sound of peace and quiet inside the entire house. All Jody really knew at that very moment was that no one had gotten shot with a gun yet. She had not heard any kind of noise. Jody guessed her daddy must have heard her scream, and then came to his senses. Maybe the sound of his daughter's voice had awakened him enough mentally to make him go into the bedroom and leave Ruby alone. Shortly thereafter, Travis must have passed out because Jody did not hear another word out of him that night. She was so thankful for the silence. She remembers her mom coming into her bedroom and massaging her shoulder for a moment, while telling her to go back to sleep.

To this day, Jody still wonders what might have happened next if she had not screamed that night. Maybe nothing would have transpired, but then again, something may have. Maybe her mom would not be here now. Jody knew that if her dad had shot her mom that night, then he may as well have shot her, too.

After this horrifying episode, Jody thanked Jesus for answering her prayer. She is sure the Lord must have spoken to her daddy's heart that night about putting the gun away. Thankfully, she has not seen him with another weapon since then. She's not even certain he still owns one. If he does, Jody says he's never taken it out inside their home again. For this reason, deep in her heart, she is convinced her daddy is very sorry for that awful night. "This makes me extremely happy," Jody says, "because I love him so much." She's made up her mind, though, that if he ever points a gun at her mom's head again, she'll get right up in his face and say, **"shoot and kill *me*."**

No Sure Winner

Surely, for certain, and of course, I swear,
Are some very strong words, you'd better beware.

D.J. DeSai

When I was twelve years old, a dollar bill was a lot more money than what it is today. Cash was also harder to come by then and, fortunately, money took a little longer to spend than it does now. Back then, my daddy, Amos, owned some race horses, and he liked betting on them occasionally. Both of my parents followed the horses very closely, and this sport had become a hobby they dearly loved. It was something enjoyable that they shared together, and it was especially fun for them when their horses would win. It was also a blessing for all of us when they would win money.

I was in the seventh grade during this time, and I was involved in many activities. Needless to say, I seldom paid much attention to the race horses. I had too many other things on my mind such as skating, music, dancing, and reading.

One day while I was sitting in my bedroom reading a book, I overheard my daddy speak a few seemingly wise words. He was in the living room talking to a couple of his buddies. Earlier, I had noticed all three men looking at a racing form. They seemed to be studying it very carefully. I listened closely as I heard my daddy tell his friends that he had a "sure winner" picked in a certain horse race that would be running that same day. He seemed to know without a doubt that this one particular horse was surely going to win.

On several occasions prior to this day, I had heard my dad speak highly of a number of horses, but I had never remembered him ever saying that one of the thoroughbreds would be a "sure winner." All I could think about was the two dollars I had saved up in my piggy bank. I quickly decided I had to bet on this outstanding horse. *There is no way I can lose,* I thought to myself. *After all, a sure winner has to mean extra money in my pocket. Maybe I can turn my two dollars into a ten dollar bill in just a couple of minutes. Maybe I can win even more than that. I'd be crazy not to go along with my daddy's bet,* I assured myself.

Since I was only twelve years old at the time, I was not old enough to place a bet myself, so after Daddy's buddies left the house, I went into the living room to ask him if I could bet my two dollars on the horse he liked so much. My dad looked down at me and grinned. He said, "Yeah, Dory, I'll take your two dollars." I quickly ran into my bedroom and got the money out of my piggy bank. I handed it over to him, so sure that I would end up with a pocket full of money. I couldn't wait!

Feeling overly excited, I didn't go far from home that day because I wanted to be there when my dad walked in the door so I could collect my winnings. It seemed like an eternity as I waited for him, dreaming of what I would do with all my extra money. I decided I would put my two dollars back into my piggy bank and spend the rest of it on something else. I was so happy that I shouted out to heaven and said, "Oh my God! Thank you!" Even though I was only twelve, I still tried to remember to acknowledge the Lord in every area of my life.

After waiting a couple more hours, I started getting restless. I wondered where in the world my daddy was. I was hoping he wasn't out spending my share of the winning money. I had all kinds of plans for it when he walked through the door later that night. My mom said the races would be over around six o'clock, but Dad didn't get home until nine that night.

The first thing I noticed when he walked in the back door was that he was staggering all over the place. I was sure he had been out celebrating his winnings but I wondered why he didn't have a big grin on his face like he normally had after he had won. *He's probably just drinking a little too much to smile,* I thought. *Oh well! It doesn't matter because I'm smiling enough for the both of us.*

Watching my dad very closely, I didn't say much to him when he first walked in. I wanted to give him a chance to sit down and relax before he got his wallet out to pay me. I also figured, eventually, he would remember to give me the money he owed me. *Surely, he won't forget something so important,* I told myself.

After several more minutes passed by, I decided I may as well go ahead and ask my dad for my money since he was not volunteering to give it to me. *Wow! I guess he must have forgotten about my two-dollar bet,* I thought. When I asked him where my money was, he looked at me with a startled look on his face. Then he nonchalantly told me that the horse didn't make it. I just stood there looking at him with a depressed look on my face. My dad told me again that the horse did not win. I felt my face drop and my heart cry. Then I felt my temper rising.

"Oh no!" I screamed out loudly to my dad. "You said the horse was a sure winner! I want my money and I want it now!" I yelled at him. My dad calmly spoke back to me as if the losing horse and the lost money was no big deal. He calmly said, "Dory, I said the horse didn't get there. That's all. Maybe we'll get 'em the next time." I stood there as mad as a hornet when all of a sudden I blurted out to him, "That's not fair, Daddy! You said the horse was going to win!" I proceeded to tell my dad angrily that I wanted my two dollars back.

Daddy slowly got up from his chair and walked over to where I was standing. Suddenly, I became a little frightened, thinking that maybe I had said way too much to my dad while using a much too strong tone in my voice. After all, he did not know that I was in the other room listening in on the conversation concerning the "sure winner" earlier that day. I thought I was in big trouble until I saw him open up his wallet. Then he started talking to me with a very sarcastic pitch in his voice. He

asked me if I really thought life was fair. I shook my head, yes. He told me that I was in for a very rude awakening because life was most certainly not fair. He went on to tell me that he would give me the two dollars back this time. He also told me if I ever bet on another horse and then cried about it if I lost, I had no business whatsoever gambling again.

Needless to say, I was very grateful to get my two dollars back and I told my daddy so. I thanked him, while explaining to him that I had heard him talking about the horse being a sure winner. He explained to me that sometimes people say things that aren't totally correct, and not to take it all so seriously.

What a lesson I had been taught! Actually, there were three lessons concerning the betting of the horse that lost that day. I was taught to never bet money I did not want to lose, especially if I was going to cry about it later. I was also taught that there are some things in life that are most certainly not fair, especially when you take words that someone says to heart, and it doesn't happen. Last but not least, I learned that when it comes to gambling, I will never get my hopes up too high, because there is one thing for sure: there is **"no sure winner."**

Demolition Daddy

Your children see all that you do,
And some things leave them feeling blue.

D.J. DeSai

Fear is something we have all felt in our lives, and sometimes it can scare the living daylights out of us, especially when we are children. I hope this story will hit the hearts of all the parents who can possibly benefit from reading it. I also hope folks will remember this story, especially if their children might be feeling afraid.

My friend Jody shared this story with me several years ago, and I would like to share it with you. Jody doesn't remember a lot about her early childhood, but this one particular day stands out in her mind as if it were only yesterday. She was around ten years old at the time this event took place, but she still remembers each and every horrific detail. It happened on a beautiful Indian summer day when she and her family were living in the country on a farm.

Travis, Jody's daddy, had been turning the whiskey bottle up again and chasing it with beer. He was staggering all over the place when Jody's mother Ruby asked him for his car keys. Ruby needed to make a run to the old country store to pick up a few groceries. After she had asked Travis at least three times for the car keys, he started cursing her, and telling her no. Travis was just drunk and needed to let Ruby know who was boss. He had a habit of this same behavior quite often when he'd been drinking.

That day Travis had brought a man named Buck home with him. Not only was Buck a good friend of Travis's, he was also his drinking buddy. Naturally, Travis was trying to show off in front of his friend by not allowing Ruby to drive the family car to the store. Saying no to Ruby was probably a power tool for Travis.

Buck offered to let Ruby drive his car to the market, but Travis had firmly told him that Ruby did not need to go anywhere. Ruby just sat there saddened by her husband's behavior. She knew Travis and Buck would be leaving the house soon to go pick up more alcohol. Jody felt so sorry for her mom.

When Travis and Buck got ready to leave the house, Buck slipped Ruby his car keys, and told her to go ahead and drive his car to the store anyway. He told her to wait to go until after they had left the house, so Travis would not see her. Buck knew it would make Travis mad, and he did not want to cause trouble for the family, but he felt sorry for Ruby because Travis was treating her so badly.

Ruby was a smart woman. She did exactly what Buck had told her to do. She waited until the two of them had left the house, and then she told Jody to get into Buck's car. She told her that they were going to the store. Jody did as her mother told her to do. She climbed in on the passenger's side. She was so glad that she and her mom were finally getting to go buy groceries, even if it was without her daddy's permission. She knew this would make her mom happy.

The two of them took off down the old winding road, driving Buck's car. They were a couple of miles away from home, where the old road came to a fork, when Jody looked up and saw her dad driving their way. He was coming from the opposite direction. He was driving his own car with Buck beside him in the passenger's seat. Jody would have bet her life that her dad was not a happy camper when he realized Ruby was driving Buck's car. Ruby knew to stop the car immediately at the fork of the road when she saw Travis coming toward her. She must have known he was very upset because he was driving quite fast.

Unexpectedly, Jody saw her dad stop his car so quickly that all she could see was a cloudy fog from the tires spinning in the pile of gravel that lay in the middle of the road. Jody's vision had become so impaired by the dust flying in the air that she could hardly see her dad's car. She could still hear the spinning of his tires, and the loud squealing and screeching of the brakes when his car finally came to a halt. *Thank God!* Jody thought. *Maybe Daddy is calming down now since the car has stopped.* Suddenly she became very worried. There was too much silence, and her dad was not getting out of the car. *Oh Lord! Is Dad mad at Mom? What is he going to do now?* Jody wondered. She was sure her dad was more than angry although she could barely see both men sitting inside his car. She was so afraid! She was sure Buck was scared too, just as her mom probably was. Jody just knew there was going to be some kind of big trouble when she finally saw the mean, disturbed look on her dad's face; she had seen this look so many times before. Yes, there was definitely going to be some kind of confrontation between her parents.

Jody will never forget the details of what happened next. Travis started backing his car up as fast and far as he could from the car that she and her mom were in, which was Buck's car. Travis's car was still within enough distance that she and her mom could see it. Jody didn't really understand at the time why her dad had backed his car up so far away from them. She was also wondering why he had backed it up so abruptly. The dust from all the gravel on the road started flying again.

All of a sudden, within a blink of an eye, Travis put the pedal to the metal. He gave his car all the gas he could give it while driving straight toward Jody and her mom. Travis's car was traveling so fast that Jody was wondering when he would slow it down. He wasn't slowing it down though. Her dad was coming straight toward them as fast as his car would go. As his car continued to get closer and closer to the car they were in, Jody remembers praying that her mom would hurry and move the car out of his way before he hit them. "Oh no!" Ruby screamed out. She didn't have enough time to move the car. "Oh my God!" Jody cried out to the Lord. Her dad was not going to stop his car for any reason. He was headed straight toward her mom's side of the car, as if he wanted to hit to kill her. Jody was hoping he would change his mind and stop, but it looked as though he were gaining even more speed. She was so scared that she must have stopped breathing for the next few seconds. They seemed to be the longest and the shortest seconds of Jody's entire life. She had never remembered being so filled with fear as she was that very moment.

Jody knew Travis was going to kill her and her mother. *We do not deserve this,* Jody thought. *I hate my dad for this! Why is he acting so crazy? Why had he drunk so much?* All she really knew for sure was that her dad wanted vengeance, and vengeance was his no matter what the cost was. The price did not seem to matter at all to him at that very moment. Jody started praying. So many thoughts were going through her head, as her dad crashed his car as hard as he could into the side of the car that she and her mom were sitting in. "Oh!" Jody gasped. She felt the hard jolt! She wondered if she were still alive. She also wondered if her mom was dead or alive. She was afraid to look at her. She was in such a state of shock.

Immediately Ruby grabbed Jody and hugged her. She looked at her daughter's entire body thoroughly to make sure she was okay. Jody silently thanked God that she and her mom were still alive. She still thanks God today that her dad's car had not hit her mom's body. She is sure the impact would have killed her. Travis had hit the part of the car between the front bumper and the driver's side. He must have purposely missed the door of the driver's side, or else they both may have been killed. Jody doesn't think her dad meant to hurt anyone, but to only scare her mom. He had done just that, too. Not only had he scared Ruby to death, but also Jody, and Buck, too.

Still sitting inside Buck's car, Jody and Ruby were screaming and crying at the same time. They were both in shock and out of control. Jody still feared her dad and what he might do next, but Ruby was madder than a hornet. Jody could see it in her eyes.

Frantically and quickly, Travis jumped out of his car, and pulled Jody out of Buck's car. Then he grabbed Ruby and pulled her out, too. He put his arms around the both of them so tightly, while checking them out to make sure they were okay. All he could say was he was so sorry over and over again, while promising Ruby he would never drink alcohol again. Jody wondered if he meant it this time.

Sure that the ordeal had scared Travis as much as it had the others, Jody was also sure she saw a teardrop fall down her dad's face while Ruby continued to scream at him. Jody cried too, while trying to block everything out of her mind. Travis turned around and apologized to Buck at least three or four times for crashing into his car. He kept telling Jody and Ruby everything would be alright, as he gently led the two of them back to his own car. Ruby was still very upset. Buck got into his car and drove away. Jody wondered if he and her dad would ever be friends again. She also wondered if her mom would forgive her dad this time. She prayed their arguing would end soon.

Travis pulled his car away from the fork of the road, asking Ruby if she still wanted to go to the store. Ruby shook her head no. Jody wondered if her mom were afraid of her dad, though she felt certain she was more disturbed than scared. After all was said and done, Jody remembers feeling so secure on their way home, believing that everything would be alright for at least that one night. She wasn't sure what might happen the next time her daddy decided to get drunk again, but for now, he was okay.

The next day Travis drove to Buck's home and took his car to get it repaired. *That is the least he can do,* Jody thought to herself. He also had to take his own car to the shop to get it fixed. That was just a couple of the consequences Travis had to pay, along with the bad memory of that day always haunting him. At least, Jody hoped it would bother him enough that he would never do it again.

Jody never did stop having nightmares about the car crash until she went to see a few of the true demolition derby car races. She thinks the fun of the real races helped to take her mind off the tragic memory of their own car crash. She says she's not sure she has ever been as terrified as she was that day her daddy played demolition derby at the fork of that old country road.

Alcohol is a sickness, and Jody is certain her dad needed help. She believes with all her heart that the alcohol was what drove him to drive his own car straight into Buck's car that day. Yes, once was definitely enough for Jody when it came to the day Travis decided to play **"Demolition Daddy."**

A Wrong or a Right to Vote

Follow what you are feeling inside,
So you won't easily change your mind.

D.J. DeSai

The day I turned eighteen years old, my daddy Amos stayed on my tail all day long, wanting me to go register to vote. Finally, I had no choice but to go do it. He was not going to let up on me until I did. Of course, I registered under the same party as my dear daddy had, because I thought he hung the moon. I looked up to him so much, thinking he knew most everything.

When Election Day rolled around, I was more than ready to go cast my vote, thanks to my daddy's nudging. He practically pushed me out the front door that morning, wanting me to go do it. I kept telling him I would vote later, but he would not hear of it. He wanted to make sure I made it there on time, so I went early in the afternoon, just to please him. I knew how much it meant to my dad, and it was not really a big deal for me to give up a few minutes of my time to make him happy. Also, I knew deep down inside it was the right thing for me to do for myself, and being old enough to vote had made me feel so grown up, which was what I had wanted to be for quite some time.

I knew without a single doubt who Daddy had voted for that morning, and I was sure that I would vote the same way he had. After all, he had diligently kept up with the politics, unlike me. As a matter of fact, he had made it very plain to just about everyone in the family for whom he would vote and why. That was one reason I looked up to my dad so much. He was very interested in what was going on all over the world, and I knew he wanted me to be that way, too. I had always wanted to please him, but sometimes it was a hard job to do, especially for an eighteen year old girl like myself. He was a very old-fashioned man, and set in his own ways. My daddy's steadfastness was accepted by everyone most of the time, but occasionally it was not. No matter what, though, I loved him.

When I arrived at the neighborhood building that afternoon, I could tell there were a lot of people inside waiting to vote, because it took several minutes for me to find a parking spot. When I walked inside and saw how long the line of voters was, I wasn't surprised. It seemed like everyone had gotten the same idea at the same time. The thought had crossed my mind to just go ahead and leave the building, and tell my daddy I had voted. He would never know the difference anyway, but I couldn't do it. My conscience started bothering me, so I figured I'd just wait it out with everyone else in line.

While waiting there for at least thirty minutes, I had the opportunity to listen to a lot of people's comments and opinions about the different candidates running for office. I also had the chance to read some political material that was lying around. It was all very educational to me.
Gee! There is so much going on in the world that I am not even completely aware of, I thought to myself. *I wonder if my daddy knows some of the pros and cons I am hearing and reading about. I can't wait to go home and share some of the issues with him. This will give us something interesting to talk about,* I thought.

When it was finally my turn to go up and get my card to vote, I wished I had registered a different way, because I decided I wanted to vote for the other party's nominees. I felt as though they were going to do so much more for the town, city, state, and country in general, versus the other side I had previously registered to vote for. I made that same comment to the lady at the desk who was giving me the card to vote. She told me that although I had registered to vote one way, I could still vote whichever way I wanted to. She said it did not matter one way or the other. I told the lady that I guessed I would just vote the same way my dad had. She made the point of telling me I was eighteen years old, and I had the right to vote for whom I wanted to. "Everyone has that right," she told me again.

I thanked her, walked into the little space provided, and pulled the curtain closed. All I could think was *I'm all alone. I'm eighteen years old. I am a woman now. I can vote for whomever I please, and this is exactly what I am going to do. No one, not even my daddy, can tell me what to do. It feels wonderful to finally be able to vote and to make an adult choice all by myself,* I thought.

After I left the building and walked to my car, I held my head up high. For the first time in my life, I felt as though I had made a very wise decision on my own without anyone else's help. I couldn't wait to drive home to tell my parents about it. They would be so proud of me, I believed.

Of course, my dad greeted me at the front door when I walked in. He smiled at me while asking me if I had voted. I told him yes, and proceeded to tell him for whom I had voted. I was getting ready to tell him the reasons why I had voted the way I did when all of a sudden he blurted out some of the ugliest curse words I had heard him speak since his engine blew up in his car. "Oh my God," I whispered to the Lord, as I looked up and saw my dad's red face filled with rage and anger. Suddenly, I heard him scream, "All you did was cancel my vote, Dory!" He was still yelling when he told me he may as well have stayed at home and not even voted. He was so annoyed with me because of who I had voted for that I never even got the chance to explain to him why I had voted the way I did.

When I walked into my bedroom to avoid my dad's fury, I wondered if I had made a mistake. He had taken my vote so personally. He had said his reason for being so upset with me was because I had cancelled his vote out by voting against him. *Wow! I had never even thought of it that way. Would my dad ever speak to me again? Would he always get mad at me if I didn't vote the same way he did?* I wondered, as I sat there sad and speechless. I asked God to help me to understand my dad's feelings.

A few minutes later my mom, Leola, walked into my bedroom and sat down beside me. She put her arm around me and told me not to worry about the way my dad was acting. She said that she had learned a long time ago not to tell him who she had voted for. She told me that he had always just assumed that she had voted the same way he did, but that wasn't always the case. She was quick to tell me to keep her comment a secret for her. She went on to tell me that I might want to think about keeping my vote a secret also. My mom told me that each person has the right to vote for whomever she pleases. If anyone wants to know who you're voting for, it's okay to say, "I'd rather not say." She said that some people think they are right about certain issues, so they try to encourage you to vote the same way they do. She went on to tell me that some folks, such as my dad, get offended and upset if others don't feel the same way they do. She said it doesn't mean those people are bad people. It just means they believe in something so strongly that they want everyone else to believe it, too.

I was so thankful for our talk. I was sure that Mom was trying to make me laugh after I thought about some of the comments she had made to me that day. I remember her saying that there had been a couple of times in the past when she couldn't decide on which candidate would do the best job, so she voted for whoever she thought looked, dressed, and acted the best. She also said her reason for this was because she knew she'd have to look at that person for the next two to four years, so she'd much rather have someone win the election who was easy on the eyes rather than someone who wasn't. The two of us got a big laugh out of that comment, but I knew Daddy would have definitely blown up all over the place if he had heard that bit of information.

While explaining to me that my dad was wrong about getting upset with me about who I had voted for, Mom was also defending him in a sense, too. I was glad of this, though, because I did not want to be upset with him no matter how wrong or right he thought he was about anything. After she explained what seemed like an earful to me, I understood my dad a lot better. It wasn't right for him to tell me who to vote for, although he thought he was right about the political issues. I was sure that he thought I knew little or nothing about politics; I really didn't know much, but it was still my own choice. Acknowledging all of these thoughts, I was able to start forgiving my dad. Besides, I have always believed that I need to forgive people no matter what, if I want to be forgiven by other people and also by God, too.

For the past several years, I have continued to do what my mom suggested. I vote but I keep it to myself. It is really no one else's business anyway. After this episode, I believe my dad eventually starting respecting my ways and my rights, too. I also believe that maybe he just needed to be put in his place by witnessing his daughter having a mind of her own, just like him.

Dad never told me he was sorry for trying to decide my vote for me, but I believe he knew he was wrong because of certain conversations and debates we never had again. I could always tell when he was truly sorry about something, though, because he would try his best to make up for it in other ways.

Before my sweet dad passed away, he still always encouraged everyone he knew to vote, including me; but the one thing I never heard him speak of again was **"a wrong or a right to vote."**

Eaten by Two Sharks

Sharks await, eager to consume
One great big piece or all of you.

D.J. DeSai

During the middle of my senior year of high school, I fell into a bad habit of cutting my English class. I had been carrying an A average so, needless to say, I felt very secure about passing. Looking back now, I think the work must have been too easy for me, so boredom could have possibly inspired me to play hooky. I realize now that cutting was a waste of my time, and that I was only cheating myself. It was a dishonest thing as well, and I have always regretted it.

I knew it was time for me to snap out of my foolishness and start staying in school, though, when I noticed the semester was closing in, and my grade average had fallen tremendously. One day while I was sitting in class, trying to figure out a way to pass, my English teacher, Miss Janis, announced that she was going to give all her students a writing project to complete. The task she was referring to would possibly keep us from failing if we participated and scored a high enough grade. Miss Janis said there would be some work involved, but it would count as eighty percent of our entire grade for the semester. The assignment was for us to write a ten-page fiction short story.

Feeling so grateful for this opportunity, I breathed a sigh of relief, because I knew I needed this credit to graduate from high school early. I couldn't wait to get out, get a part-time job, and go to college, too. It was my own fault, though, that I was flunking, because the only reason for my low grade was my absence from class. I couldn't believe I had created a situation as silly as this.

Miss Janis went on to say that she was giving her pupils a certain amount of time to write the short stories. She also said we could turn them in early if we chose. I knew I had plenty of time to complete it, but I decided to get on the ball immediately. First off, I needed to think of something very interesting to write about, because I knew I had to score high enough to bring my grade back up to passing.

While sitting in my English class, remembering a story that I had read in the Bible as a child, I decided to write my assignment about being stranded alone out in the deep blue sea. I called my short story, "Eaten by a Shark."

In my story, "Eaten by a Shark," I had been swallowed up whole by a huge sea monster. During this horrific episode, I must have passed out in the midst of struggling with the shark while trying to escape his wrath. When I awakened, I was lying inside his extremely large belly. Surprisingly, I wasn't hurt at all. Soon, after I had rested and my fear had subsided, I found myself happier than I had ever been in my entire life. Feeling peaceful and content where I was, I became so excited and eager to start working on the new home that I had grown to love so very much. I used all the internal parts of the shark's belly for my furniture while contemplating the décor of the many walls that surrounded me. *How wonderful!* I thought. *My "home sweet home" has great potential*, I smiled to myself.

Anxious to start decorating everything the way I had imagined it, I started exploring into the deepest parts of the shark's body. *Wow!* I thought. I found so many loose, odd, and interesting shaped bones, shells, and other jewel-like sea treasures that I knew I could use to design my new home as beautifully as I could. Soon, with a touch of my artistic imagination and my two hands, my home became very cozy inside. I was so proud of my new palace.

The food that I found myself eating inside my new home was extraordinarily delicious and healthy. Of course, my daily menu would depend on what the shark ate, which was almost always very tasty seafood. I was completely satisfied after each meal, and I felt more comfortable and safe than I ever had before. One thing was for sure: no one was going to harm my home, because the shark was considered a dangerous species. After all, he had consumed all of me in one single gulp. This thought made me feel very secure in my blessed home.

My most peaceful resting time inside the shark's belly was when he would soar like an eagle through the beautiful blue sea. The ride was nothing but smooth sailing, and so relaxing for me. I could fall asleep and wake up feeling so refreshed, as the shark glided through the water. I also loved looking at all the scenic beauty when the shark opened up his mouth and gills. I was in awe. It was so amazing to me how all the sea creatures lived. I had learned so much, but I wondered if I would ever be able to tell about it. I didn't really care, though, because I was so happy in my new-found home that I never wanted to leave.

One day, however, the shark ate something that did not agree with him, and shortly thereafter, he became very ill. He started vomiting from his sickness. Lo and behold, he threw me up too! I found myself traveling at high speed as he shot me like a bullet right out of his mouth. Soon, I was swimming around in the cold, salty water just as I had before he found me. Yes, he had spat me up with all the other food that had made him sick. My happy little home had quickly exploded out into the water like a stick of dynamite. My heart was so saddened from losing everything I had fallen in love with. *What in the world will I do now?* I wondered, as I swam around in the water looking for my shark. He had disappeared so quickly that I found myself seeking new shelter. Suddenly, I felt sick, too. I couldn't help but wonder if I were feeling bad from what the shark had eaten, or if it was because I had lost my wonderful home.

Thank God, a few minutes later I was rescued by a huge ship that was cruising out in the sea. I was very thankful for the crew's help, although I still felt so lonely and empty inside. I missed my place of paradise that I had decorated so nicely, while I hoped and prayed the shark was alive and well, too.

After thinking seriously about all that I had lost, I decided there was a lot that I would always hold close to my heart, too. I had so many wonderful memories of the shark, and I would cherish them for the rest of my life. This was "the end" of my ten-page fiction short story called, "Eaten by a Shark."

The next day I went to school and turned my short story in to my English teacher, Miss Janis. I still had another week left before the deadline, but I had finished it early, feeling sure I had written it as well as I knew how to. All I could hope and pray for now was that my teacher would love my shark story enough to give me a passing grade.

A couple of days later, Miss Janis asked me to stay after class. She told me she needed to talk to me about something very important. *Oh no!* I thought to myself. *I must have made a bad grade!* I was so worried during the entire class, wondering what in the world could be wrong with the assignment I had written. *Miss Janis must have hated my story,* I kept thinking to myself. *It was probably too far-fetched.* I only wanted to pass, but I was so scared now that I had failed. Why else in the world would my teacher ask me to stay after class? I started praying, asking God for help.

After the bell rang and the rest of the students had left the classroom, I walked up to Miss Janis's desk. My hands were shaking and my knees were weak. I was really scared! Thankfully, my teacher didn't waste any time reaching inside her drawer to pull out my short story. She laid it down on the table face up so that I could plainly see it. "Oh my God! Thank you Lord!" I shouted. I could not believe my eyes. There was an A+ written on the top of the first page. I felt so surprised and very, very flattered. My grade was beautiful. I was so grateful.

Before I had turned my story in, I'd been thinking that maybe it was "just okay." The last thing I had expected was to get an A+ on it. Miss Janis told me that she was very proud of my paper and of me. She told me that my short story was one of the best she'd ever read by one of her students. She also told me to never stop writing, because this was surely my talent. The teacher said I had been blessed with a God-given gift, to always pursue it, and to never give up on it. Miss Janis asked me some other questions, and then complimented my writing some more. I walked out of the room that day feeling like I was on cloud nine and no one could bring me down. I felt so good about my grade that I believed anything was possible now.

Meanwhile, there was a guy named Fritz in my English class. I had always felt sorry for him, because several of my classmates called him bad names and made fun of him. They really started harassing him when they found out he did not have a story written to turn in. They all told him he was going to fail the class, making rude and snide remarks to him about his being dumb and stupid. I felt so sorry for him and wished I could help him.

One day I saw Fritz standing in the hallway. I couldn't help but stop and ask him why he had not written a short story. He told me he could not think of anything to write about. I told him there were lots of subjects he could choose, and it did not matter what it was. Fritz said he did not understand what fiction meant, so I explained it to him. I told him it was something made-up and not true. I showed him the unbelievable story I had written about making my home in a shark's belly. Fritz told me he thought my story was cool, and then asked me if he could read it. He said that maybe he could understand how to write his story after he read mine. I did not have the time to wait for Fritz to read my entire ten page story, so I told him to take it home with him. I told him to read it and bring it back to me the next day. Fritz thanked me as he placed my assignment in his folder. He thanked me again when we said goodbye. It made me feel good just to know I was helping someone who everyone had called stupid. I was hoping that he would make an A+ just as I had, and then surprise the heck out of all our other classmates.

The next day Fritz kept his promise. He brought my short story back to me. When he handed it to me, I asked him if he had written a story, and he said yes. I told him I had known all along that he could do it, and I was very proud of him. He dropped his head, as if he was embarrassed. As he quickly walked away, I believed in my heart that there must be hope for every one, even Fritz.

A couple of days later, Miss Janis asked me to stay after class again. She said she needed to discuss something very important with me. I smiled and told her okay. I was sure that she only wanted to praise my story again, and I most certainly did not mind that at all. It made me feel so good just knowing that someone else loved my writing, especially Miss Janis.

Feeling overly confident this time, I walked up to my teacher's desk after all the other students had left the classroom. I was far from feeling nervous while waiting for another compliment concerning my work. Suddenly, I became a little worried. Miss Janis did not look as happy as she had before. She looked at me with a very hurt and disturbed look on her face. Then she said, "Dory, I am very disappointed in you for allowing another student to copy the ten page story you wrote." She went on to say that she had no choice but to flunk us both. I was flabbergasted! For a moment, I stood there in shock not knowing what in the world to say. I couldn't believe what I had just heard. Suddenly, I spoke up. I was quick to tell my teacher no, that I had certainly not let anyone else copy my story. Miss Janis just shrugged her shoulders, while showing me the replica of my own ten page story. The story had Fritz's name written on the first page.

"Oh no!" I cried to Miss Janis. All I could do was cover my face while trying to wipe away the river of tears that were falling from my eyes. Fritz was the guy who everyone had called stupid, and he had copied my shark story without changing one single word. *All the other classmates are right about him,* I thought silently. *He really is stupid! There is no hope for him,* I assured myself. I could not believe that he had cheated me after I had only tried to help him. I was so hurt that I could barely maintain my composure by then. I stood there and wept over my A+ that had quickly turned into an F, and only because I had chosen to help someone.

Miss Janis handed me some tissues to wipe my eyes and face. Through my tears, as best as I knew how to, I started explaining what had happened. I told her how I had only tried to be nice to someone who so many of the other classmates had made fun of. Now, because he had done me so wrong, I was the one who would have to pay the consequences for it.

Still sobbing uncontrollably, I told Miss Janis that I would never help anyone again. I told her that I was so sorry I had tried to be kind to someone who had turned out to be nothing but a big bad shark himself. I must have really let my emotions show because, the next thing I knew, Miss Janis was standing next to me trying to console me. My teacher told me she believed what I was saying and had changed her mind about my grade. She told me she was not going to take the A+ away from me, because I deserved it, but she would be sure to flunk Fritz for copying my story. She also told me to be very careful in the future when trusting someone with my work. She said it is very important to always use discretion.

I knew what Miss Janis was talking about. It was alright for me to encourage Fritz to do his assignment, but I was wrong to let him take my story home with him. No matter what, though, I had learned a big lesson, and I would know better the next time. I thanked Miss Janis with all of my heart for giving me the A+ back.

As I left the classroom that day feeling a little vulnerable, I also felt so much more mature. I decided not to say anything to Fritz about what had happened. He would find out soon enough anyway; plus, he knew what he had done was very wrong. I had also decided that I was not very smart myself for letting him take my story home with him. Honestly, though, the thought never crossed my mind that he would actually copy it word for word. *Who would be that stupid?* I wondered. And after all was said and done, he never even apologized to me. *What a guy!* I reminded myself.

Still, to this day, I can't help but believe that Fritz most certainly did act as a shark himself for copying my story, "Eaten by a Shark." Although I have forgiven him for it, he was ready and willing to devour me by stealing from me. He did steal my story, and he almost managed to steal my A+. One thing I can say for sure now is this: I definitely know what it feels like to be **"eaten by two sharks."**

Toilet Dunk

Just because you want a friend,
Don't start a fight you cannot win.

D.J. DeSai

When I was a seventh grader, going to middle school, I met the guy who I thought was the love of my life. He was a senior in high school, and his name was Ben. He and I were enrolled in the same school, and we soon started going steady a few weeks after we met. I was on cloud nine as Ben's girlfriend, and everyone at school knew I was so happy.

I also had a lot of girlfriends in my classes. One girl, though, acted as my enemy. This certain person seemed to be out to get me. She would make snide remarks to me, making every effort to put me down in front of other people. I didn't really know who this girl was other than she was a classmate of mine. I had a strange feeling, though, that I was about to get to know her soon enough. Her name was Joy.

One day in the midst of changing classes, Joy followed me and Ben down the hallway, yelling nasty comments to me. At first I just ignored her, but it didn't seem to matter: Joy only continued, and her verbal abuse was just getting worse. She had made up her mind to be nothing but a thorn in my side, and there was nothing I could do about it. As a matter of fact, I was starting to look helpless in front of my boyfriend Ben, my girlfriends, and all the other classmates. After all, Joy was doing all of the name calling, and I was not firing back at her in any way, shape, or form. I was only trying to be lady-like in front of everyone.

It didn't take long for all the other students in the hallway to turn around with surprised looks on their faces as Joy shouted out intimidating comments to me. Joy's voice was extremely loud, and her words sounded so obnoxious. Before I could even defend myself, she called me a bitch. By this time, Ben and I had stopped and turned around to face Joy in the hallway. My face turned bright red from the embarrassment of being humiliated in front of everyone. I couldn't believe it! I had never even spoken to this girl before and now she was calling me this horrible name. *How much more degrading could she possibly be?* I asked myself.

Suddenly, I became so angry. I looked Joy directly in the eye and said, "It takes one to call one!" I was hoping my bravery would discourage her from any more vulgar talk, but it didn't work. Joy was still screaming at the top of her lungs while telling me to meet her in the restroom at a certain time that same day. She said we would settle the score then. I agreed with Joy, only to let her know I wasn't afraid of her, but the last thing I really wanted to do was fight with a girl I didn't even know. I wondered why Joy was so mad at me. I also wondered why in the world she wanted to fight. All I really knew was I had to meet her there. I could not and would not let her think for one single minute that I was scared of her, although I really was fearful to an extent. I had never fought with anyone except my three brothers. I was sure that my tomboy fighting did not mean a thing when it came to fighting with a girl. I did not have a sister, so I didn't have a clue as to what would happen in the restroom that day. I felt nothing but anxiety.

When it was time to meet Joy, I wondered if I should just run away. I didn't want to follow through with this fight, but I was smart enough to know I couldn't be a coward either. As crazy as it may sound, everyone at school had their eyes and ears set straight on this feud. Again, it was not what I wanted, but Joy was never going to leave me alone if I were to back down now. This was the main reason I knew I had to show up.

The appointment went as planned. I was followed down the hallway and into the restroom by several other girlfriends of mine that wouldn't have missed this fight for anything in the world. There were also a few guys, including Ben, standing in the hallway outside the restroom. I was feeling nervous and nauseous, but I was more than ready to get this fight over with.

As soon as I opened the restroom door, I saw Joy and a couple of other girls standing there talking. I walked right up to Joy with as much gumption as I could possibly show and said, "Well, here I am." Joy said, "Yeah, come on bitch. Let's do it." I told her to go ahead and do whatever it was she wanted to do. Joy said, "Come on and hit me." I said, "I don't want to hit you." I reminded Joy that she was the one who had started the fight and then called me to the restroom for a reason I did not even understand.

Still desiring to show off her courageous personality, Joy called me a bitch again, while shoving my shoulder. Needless to say, her behavior was agitating me extremely. Finally, I was ready to give her a taste of her own medicine. Her bullying had taken its toll on me, and I had taken all that I was going to take from her. I had tried to be civil to my foe, but it just wasn't working.

Before Joy had a chance to shove me again, I quickly grabbed her arms, and easily twisted her entire body around like a paper doll. Gee! She was nothing but skin and bones! I was holding on to her so tightly that she wasn't able to move a muscle. It was amazing! Joy was all talk with little or no physical strength at all. It didn't take a lot of energy for me to hold her in place. The only problem I was having was that I didn't know what in the world to do with my enemy. I started to loosen up on her but as soon as I did, she got her hands loose, and started waving them in my face. This only irritated me more. Joy was starting to get a little crazy with her flapping hands, so I grabbed her again in a somewhat violent manner. Her blouse started ripping, and it didn't take long for her buttons to start falling off. I didn't really want to hurt Joy, but she was still trying to throw baby smacks toward my face. I knew she was not going to give up on this fight of hers, so daringly I decided to put a scare into her. I grabbed her a lot tighter, and then put her in a head lock. I had one hand around her neck, so she wasn't going anywhere. Then I pinched her face with my other hand, using some force. All she was doing was screaming loudly. She couldn't get loose.

Quickly, I looked around for a place to put Joy's head, since I was holding on to it so tightly. I knew if I let her go again, she would come right back at me using her hands. Good grief! I didn't know what to do with her. I was all out of ideas. I could hear several voices in the restroom laughing and yelling, telling me to beat the crap out of Joy. I thought about punching her in her face a couple of times, but I couldn't find that kind of meanness in my heart. I also did not want to let her get away with anything either. I wanted to teach her a lesson. I still had her in a head lock, so I decided the safest and classiest thing left to do with her was to lead her entire body to the restroom stall while holding on to her face.

After I got Joy to the front of the toilet, she was acting so feisty from her waist down that I almost lost the head lock. I knew I had to act fast, so I decided to put her entire face and head inside the toilet bowl. I was getting ready to dunk Joy's head into the nasty water when I suddenly heard a sharp voice from behind me say, "Let her up now or you'll be expelled from school. I said you'd better let the girl go right now." I also felt someone's firm hand on my shoulder, trying to pull me away from Joy.

When I turned around to see who had spoken to me, I saw the librarian standing there. I knew I'd better listen to her, but I stood there for one moment longer so I would be sure to let Joy know who had won the fight. When I let her head up from the toilet bowl, I saw blood smears on her blouse. Then I saw blood trickling down her face, and her eyes were swollen, too. Joy's hair was one complete mess, and I almost felt sorry for her for just one split second. That feeling quickly changed, though, when I remembered that she was the one who had caused all the trouble from the beginning.

All of my girlfriends were standing there trying not to laugh their tails off while telling the librarian that Joy had started the entire fight with me. Thankfully, the other girls also told the librarian that I was only taking up for myself. I looked in the mirror and didn't think I looked any different than I had before I walked into the restroom. Poor Joy! Her clothing was falling off her, and she definitely looked like she had been in a fight. I wondered if she were sorry she had started the entire ordeal.

After I was given a verbal warning from the librarian, I walked away. I felt as though I had gotten off easy from fighting in the restroom. I never did find out what Joy's punishment was, but I was sure she must have suffered enough from just knowing that everyone else had seen her lose the fight.

I remember exactly what Joy said to me in class the next day when she sat down beside me. She told me that she had fought plenty of other girls before, but she had never fought anyone as strong as I was. Joy also told me she wanted to be my friend, and this was the reason why she had called the fight with me. "Dory, it was my only way of getting your attention," Joy said. *Oh my God,* I silently prayed. "You could have gotten my attention a lot easier by simply saying hello or by being nice to me," I told her.

The next words that came out of Joy's mouth were breath-taking for me. I couldn't believe it when she asked me if I would help her fight other girls in the future. I was very quick to tell Joy no. I told her it wasn't my nature to start fights, nor did I have the desire to do so. Joy told me that I could probably whip most of the girls in school, because she'd never seen a girl fight like me before. She also told me that she never wanted to fight me again after being whipped by me. Then, thankfully, Joy said she probably should give up fighting all together. I told her those were the smartest words I had heard her say yet.

I had never thought of myself as being strong, although I had always been called a tomboy by most of my family members. Growing up with three brothers and trying to keep up with them had never been an easy task for me. I was guessing, though, that it had paid off in the restroom that day. My brothers had made me very strong from all their wrestling rounds they had invited me to participate in.

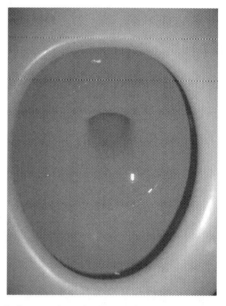

Looking back now, there is one thought that fills my heart with happiness concerning the fight with Joy that day. It is the encouraging possibility that my new-found friend has decided to stop starting fights with other people. I wonder if some of that bold and punk behavior inside Joy finally disappeared from the fight in the restroom that day. And who would think that a girl like her might be changed by just one **"toilet dunk?"**

Saved by the Hood Ornament

Reach out for something to hold on to;
You just never know, it might save you.

D.J. DeSai

I have often heard it said that if you lose your health, you have nothing. I believe if you lose your life, and you have not accepted Jesus in your heart, the loss of eternal life is far worse than a loss of health. Wouldn't it be better to lose your health in this life, than to lose the gift of eternal life in heaven after death? I feel so blessed to have my good health here on this earth, but I also think there would be nothing worse than to lose the gift of eternal life in heaven.

The prayer to heaven is so simple. You give your whole heart to Jesus, believing that he came to earth and died on the cross for your sins, and then you ask him to forgive you of your sins. We were all born sinners, but the forgiveness of sins through Christ Jesus is the first step to receiving eternal life. I love the Bible Scripture that says, *What profits a man if he gains the whole world, but loses his own soul?* These are some words that I have often thought about ever since the incident in this story took place several years ago. I saw my life on earth flash before me in one split second.

When I was thirteen years old, I was struck by a vehicle. It happened on a foggy, cloudy, rainy day when I unintentionally stepped out in front of a moving car. My mom, Leola, had driven to a neighborhood laundromat that day to wash and dry clothes because the family's washing machine had broken down. Mom had taken me with her, along with my best friend, Jody, who lived next door.

After sitting inside the hot and muggy laundromat for about an hour, I asked my mom if Jody and I could walk across the street to a drugstore to buy a soda and snack. She gave us permission to go. Instead of the two of us walking to the stoplight and waiting for the signal, we walked straight to the sidewalk and then proceeded to cross the street. Each side of the road consisted of three lanes, and as soon as the traffic in two of the lanes had come to a complete stop, I just assumed the stoplight had turned red and it was clear to cross.

While talking a mile a minute to Jody, I was not watching the traffic that was still moving fast in the inside lane. The speed limit was forty-five miles an hour, and the street was very wet that day from a misty, warm rain that had been falling for most of the morning and afternoon.

Illegally, Jody and I started crossing the street when all of a sudden we heard the sudden, harsh, and shrill sound of tires squealing. At that very same moment, I quickly realized that I would soon be struck by the car that was trying to stop so suddenly. I heard Jody scream as loudly as she could at the top of her lungs. She yelled, "Watch out, Dory!" My only prayer was, *Oh my God! Help me!* Within that same split second, my left

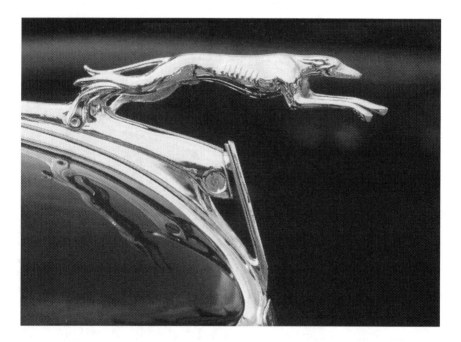

hand fell directly on top of the hood ornament on the moving car. I tightly grabbed hold of it, feeling as though an angel had firmly placed my hand on the trinket, only for me to grasp it. It felt so natural to me, holding on to the ornament for as long as I could. The time frame couldn't have been any longer than that same split second, although it seemed like it had. Yes, my fingers had encircled the trinket securely, allowing me to hold on to it as if it were meant to be there to steady and slow my body down from what was about to happen next. I was getting ready to feel the full-fledged blow of the moving car. The only thought that penetrated deep into my mind at that very moment was *this must be an act of God*. I could not believe this was really happening to me, nor can I believe it to this very day.

The moving car hit me so suddenly and the thrust was so powerful that it sent my entire body sliding down the street on the sides of my shoes. I never did fall completely down on the road, nor did I hit the asphalt with any part of my body. I stayed up on my feet. My feet were tilted, almost as if I were on roller skates making a sharp turn. I remember hearing and feeling a very hard thud, as the car hit me directly on my left side, showing no mercy whatsoever. I could not believe my feet could slide so smoothly down the wet road. It was almost as if I were wearing my socks on a newly finished waxed floor. Yes, I was sliding sideways on the sides of my feet and shoes, and there was no time to think about anything else except where I was going and where I would end up.

After it was over, I don't remember leaving the road. I'm sure I did though, because I ended up on the sidewalk with or without the help of my friend Jody and the driver of the car. The man who had hit me was nice enough or scared enough to ask me if I was okay. I don't really recall what I said to him because I only remember trying to breathe. The hard blow had knocked the breath completely out of me and my body must have gone into a state of shock.

Immediately after the accident, the last thing that should have been on my mind was being afraid that my mother had seen the accident and would never trust me to walk to the store again. I wanted my independence so badly, and if my mom found out that I had been hit by a vehicle, she would continue to shelter me more than she already had in the past. I did not want this. I wanted to grow up. I couldn't wait to move out and be on my own. Of course, I wondered if I *should* even be trusted. I was so busy talking that I had walked right out in front of a moving car. *What in the world was I thinking?* I asked myself. *That was the problem. I wasn't thinking at all.*

Again, I just assumed that all of the cars in all three lanes had come to a halt, but they had not. The traffic in the center lane was still moving at a steady flow. *Oh well! I learned a huge lesson,* I thought. I made a solemn promise to always walk to the crosswalk, and never take the moving traffic for granted again. I would be extra careful from now on. My body was hurting badly, and I was so sorry I had been so careless.

I don't really recall all the details of what happened next, except I do remember the man getting back into his car and driving off without saying another word to me. He was probably too worried to stick around. I believe Jody and I walked back into the laundromat and sat down, because I was still having trouble breathing. I remember telling my friend that I did not want her to tell my mom about the accident. I told her if she did, my mom would never allow me to go anywhere with her again. Jody promised me that she would not tell her. I knew my secret was safe with her. My only concern now was my aching body.

The next day I had to get up and go to school. I remember being so sore that I could hardly get out of bed. It was also very difficult for me to dress myself. I could hardly walk. I thought about staying home, but I loved school and didn't want to miss it. I also did not want my parents to find out that I was hurt. Yes, I was definitely injured. The entire left side of my body was swollen. It was also covered with the biggest, blackest, bluest bruise I had ever seen in my life. Vertically, the bruise covered the top left side of my breast all the way down to my hip. The bruise also ran horizontally from the middle of my stomach all the way across the middle of my back. There was also swelling and bruising at the top of my leg. I was a complete mess. It frightened me just to look at myself in the mirror.

During school that day, my body hurt me so badly that when it was time for my gym class, I could hardly move. When my teacher told me it was my turn to get up and jump on the trampoline, I told her I couldn't. The gym teacher was quick to tell me that I most certainly would have to jump because everyone else had to. I stood there not knowing what to say or do, but knowing for sure my body would not allow me to jump on the trampoline. The teacher was getting frustrated with me, telling me that I was holding up the entire class. Again, she said I had to participate, and she would wait all day if she had to. She told me to hurry up and get a move on.

Still, I just stood there knowing that if I told my teacher what was wrong, she might give my secret away. I did not want this. Not only did I not want my parents to find out about the car accident, I felt silly for what had happened. I was embarrassed that I had walked right out in front of a moving car. I just wanted to forget about the painful ordeal.

Reluctantly, one of my classmates softly spoke up and told the gym teacher that I had been hit by a car and had a big bruise on my side. My classmate went on to tell her that this was the reason why I could not jump. The teacher immediately walked over to me and pulled my top up. I saw her mouth and her eyes open up wide. Her expression changed as if she could not believe what she was looking at. "Oh my!" she shouted, as she sympathetically asked me why I had not told her I was so badly hurt. I told her I did not want to be sent home and that I would be okay. I also told my teacher I was sorry because I couldn't jump on the trampoline. I told her I would jump the next day. My gym teacher said, "Oh no, sweetie; that's okay. You don't have to jump on the trampoline until you're completely healed." She asked me if my parents knew about the car accident. Needless to say, I lied and told her, yes. The teacher told me I had her permission to go on home if I wanted to. I told her I didn't want to go home. "Besides, the day is almost over," I reminded her. The teacher agreed, and told me to let her know if I needed anything.

Thankfully, my body healed several weeks later, and not one single person in my family found out that I was hit by a car that day. When I think about the horrible event now, I realize I most certainly should have told my parents every single detail concerning my wounds. I could have been seriously injured internally too, and in need of medical attention.

Back then, I was young and immature. I also thought I was invincible, as many other teenagers feel they are now. I didn't take getting struck by a car seriously enough, and that was surely not a good thing. I was blessed, but not telling my parents about the accident could have been a matter of life and death. I want to stress the importance of revealing the truth concerning all injuries that anyone may have in the future.

Still, to this day, I can't help but think about the hood ornament on top of the car that hit me. I truly believe it was there for me, and the accident was nothing more than an act of God to wake me up. I was being much too careless. I also know that I was saved by the rain that day, too. The wet road had paved my way. It had caused my feet to slide so smoothly, instead of allowing my entire body to do flip flops or cartwheels down the highway on the asphalt. Yes, there is no doubt about it. God protected me, and I thank him with all my heart for making sure I was **"saved by the hood ornament."**

Someone Your Own Size

Pick on someone your own size,
Or you might win the chicken prize.

D.J. DeSai

Fear is not one of my favorite feelings. I'd much rather be happy-go-lucky all the time, but who gets to pick and choose how she wants to feel? I compare fear to a bolt of lightning, because we never know when it's going to strike. If someone told us that it would surely strike us, then we might choose to run and hide, just as I wanted to do in this story.

Jody lived next door to me, and we were best friends. We were also the same age. Every morning we would walk to school together, and every afternoon we would walk home together. It was about a fifteen-minute walk. After school would let out each day, the two of us would meet at the front door and then head for home. I was thankful to have my best friend living next door to me so we could walk together. There was no neighborhood bus for us to ride, because we lived so close to our school.

Our walk every morning was usually nice. It didn't matter to us if it were hot, cold, wet, or dry. We had each other to talk and laugh with while on our way. On the other hand, our walk from school to home was a lot different. There were two older girls who always liked picking on us, and they would really scare us. They were about two or three years older, and several inches taller than we were. They were really big-boned girls, too. It didn't seem fair that the older girls bugged us all the time. I had always thought they should pick on someone their own size.

These two monster girls would usually lag behind me and Jody every day, but when they would spot us ahead of them, they would start walking as fast as they could to catch us. They would get as close behind us as they could, and then they would start kicking the heels of our shoes, trying to trip us. They could really kick hard, too. Then the two big bullies would start calling us bad names while shoving us around. They would push us, knock our books out of our hands, and laugh at us. Sometimes Jody and I would start crying, so the older girls would finally leave us alone. It was so frustrating! Needless to say, we disliked the older girls, but more than that, we hated the way they always badgered us.

One day Jody was too sick to go to school. I did not mind walking alone that morning, but all I could think about all day long was how I could dodge the two big girls on my way home from school. I knew Jody could not protect me from them, but I still felt a little safer just knowing my friend and I would be taking the abuse together, versus taking it all by my lonesome self.

After school that day, I tried to bide some time. I waited around in the hallway for awhile, hoping the two trouble makers had already gone home. I figured an extra ten minutes of goofing around would throw them off my path. I was hoping they were clear out of my sight before I left the school.

While walking home, I had a feeling I should have waited an extra twenty minutes. When I got about halfway down the road, I heard their shrill voices echoing from behind me. I turned around to see where they were, as I heard them laughing out loud and walking as fast as they could to catch me. I didn't think they were too far from me, and I was right. "Oh my God! Help me Jesus!" I cried out, as my heart started pounding faster and harder. All I could do was pray. *Maybe I can beat them home before they catch up with me,* I hoped. I immediately started walking as fast as my skinny legs would go, but I could hear their nasty voices getting closer to me as every single second passed. I knew I had lost the game, and my heart began to sink. "I don't have a chance!" I whispered to myself. The more I thought about their abuse, the more nervous I became. The more nervous I became, the more adrenaline I felt. By the time the gigantic girls had made their way to me, I was ready for them, or at least I thought I was. I was feeling nothing but driven by then!

The two mean girls walked up from behind me, but before they could start their kicking and shoving, I turned around and started yelling at the top of my lungs. I don't even remember everything I said to them, but the one line I kept screaming out was, "Why don't you two pick on someone your own size?" I was ready to fight both of them at the same time, no matter what the consequences might be. I thought I'd save the girls their time, so I went ahead and threw all my books down on the sidewalk as hard as I could. Then I pointed both my fists up in the air. *Wow!* I thought. From the looks on both girls' faces, I was sure I must have scared, shocked, or surprised the heck out of them. They looked at me like I was some kind of crazy person. Then they looked at each other and one of the girls said, "Oh, come on, let's go; she's not worth our time." They both fled from me in a hurry. They walked away as fast as they could and left me standing there wondering what in the world had happened.

I stood up to both those big girls that day, and it had worked. They took off and didn't bother me at all anymore. I could not believe it! I couldn't wait to get home to tell Jody what had happened. Of course, she didn't believe me when I told her, but I sure made a believer out of her when the two girls never bothered us again. They would still continue to pass me and Jody as they walked home from school, but the only communication we received from the two intimidators was rude comments. They would say, "Better leave that little girl alone or she'll throw a fit!" or "We'd better get out of that crazy girl's way!" It made no difference to me, though. I didn't care what comments they made, as long as they continued to leave us alone physically.

Several years later, I was buying gas at a neighborhood station when I looked over and saw one of the girls. She was pumping gas, too. She was right beside me. I don't know what in the world came over me, but I knew I had to make a comment to the girl. I yelled over at her and asked her where her side-kicking buddy was. The big girl looked at me and turned away as if she were so embarrassed and scared. She had to know who I was. I yelled at her again and told her that I was all grown up now and asked her if she were going to kick my heels again. "My name is Dory, and what goes around comes around!" I screamed at her.

I didn't really want to pick a fight with the girl. I just wanted her to know how I had felt years ago. I was only trying to give her a taste of her own medicine, but it really wasn't the same thing. Those big girls had picked on Jody and I, and they were so much older. I was so scared back then, but not now! Now, I was the same size as she was, although the girl was still a much bigger-boned person than I. It didn't matter though. Our size differences were nothing compared to what they were in school.

Maybe I just wanted some kind of response or apology from her, or maybe I needed to put a closure on the entire ordeal. It didn't matter much anyhow. The big girl was not going to budge. She was hurrying around so fast, trying to finish pumping her gas so she could get the heck out of Dodge. I could relate. I knew that feeling so well. That's exactly how the girls had made Jody and I feel many years ago.

Tastefully and graciously, I decided to put my own closure on the situation. I tried to choose my words very carefully when I softly yelled at the lady one last time and said, "Hey! I have something to say to you. I'm not a fighter; I love the Lord. I'm also a very firm believer that you shouldn't harass other people. If you're going to be a red-neck, though, and pick on someone, you should pick on **'someone your own size.'**"

Two Derby Jackpots

When the odds are high, and you think you can't win,
Be careful that you don't let fear set in.

D.J. DeSai

It wasn't just an ordinary day in Louisville, Kentucky. It was Derby Day, and I could feel the excitement soaring in the air. Everyone seemed to be in a great mood as people crowded into the city in cars, trucks, buses, and planes. I could also see folks walking on almost every street.

As much as I hated going to work that day, I had to. I needed the money and the business I worked for needed me. Needless to say, I would not be going to the Derby, but I would be sure to watch the big race on television that afternoon when I arrived home.

That day at work, my boss, Alex, cut out some small pieces of paper from the daily newspaper. Then he carefully folded them all up, and dropped them into a small plastic glass. This would become his Derby jackpot. Usually, there would be around twenty horses' names in the pot. The jackpot was a tradition every year at the business, and I was so glad because this was something I looked forward to. Since I couldn't go to the Derby, drawing a horse to pull for was the next best thing.

After a few of the customers and employees had drawn a horse, Alex brought the glass over for me to draw one. I paid my dollar to him, and then slowly pulled one piece of paper out. I unfolded the paper and looked at my horses' name and wondered how I should pronounce it. *This is an unusual name,* I thought to myself. The first words that came out of my mouth were, "Oh no! I've never heard of this horse before." Anyone could have seen the excitement in my face suddenly fade away. I was so disappointed in my draw. I glanced at my co-workers and said, "Gee! I must have drawn a very bad horse." Everyone started laughing at my comment. It may have been funny to them, but not to me. I wished I could draw another one, but I didn't want to be a horse hog. There were still other people who would probably want to draw before the day was over. I was quick to tell Alex that if there were any left over, I wanted to buy another one. Alex grinned and said, "Yes, Dory, I will keep that in mind."

A few minutes later, Jack, one of my regular customers came in. While I was talking to him, he saw one of the other co-workers draw a ticket from the jackpot. Jack asked me if he could draw one out, too. I told him yes. I walked over and asked Alex if there were any tickets left. He told me he had one more left in the glass. I took the glass to my client, put his dollar bill in the envelope and let him draw out the last ticket. I watched as Jack opened up his paper. "Wow! I drew the favorite horse pick of the race!" Jack yelled. I half-way grinned at my client and said, "Good for you." I was happy for Jack, but sad for myself. I hated the horse I had drawn out of the jackpot, but there was nothing I could do about it. There were no more tickets left.

As I stood there chatting with Jack about the horse he had drawn, I jokingly asked him if he'd like to trade with me. He laughed out loud and said, "Yeah, right!" I courteously laughed back, still wishing I could have drawn one of the better choices of horses in the big Derby race. Anxiously, I yelled out to all my other co-workers, asking if anyone else wanted to trade with me. No one volunteered. They all started laughing at me again, making big fun of the horse I had drawn. I decided I'd be better off to just keep quiet the rest of the day. I didn't want to be teased anymore.

Finally, the work day was over, and I headed for home. I walked through the door about an hour before the Derby race was to be televised. After I changed my clothes and was getting ready to turn on the television, I heard my phone ring. When I answered it, I heard Beth, my mother-in-law on the other end. Beth said hello to me and asked me how my day was going. I told her it was just okay, and that I was getting ready to watch the big horse race. She told me she was doing the same thing. She went on to say that she had made a Derby jackpot earlier, and asked me if I would like for her to draw a ticket out for me. Beth told me she only had one left. She also told me if I wanted one, she would put my dollar in the pot and I could pay her for it later.

Suddenly, I became so excited! "Yes!" I screamed. "I'd love one!" Beth laughed out loud and said, "Okay, Dory. Let me open this up and see which horse is yours." I sat there silently waiting for what I was hoping to be one of the favorite horse picks in the race. *Just maybe I will get lucky this time,* I thought. Beth said, "Alright, Dory. Your horse is named Ferdinand." "Oh my," I sighed, feeling so much disappointment. "That's the same horse I drew out of the jackpot at work," I told her. Beth just laughed at my comment, as everyone else had that day. She wished me good luck as we hung up the phones.

As more displeasure fell all over me, I would have bet a million dollars that my two jackpot draws were not worth a dime. The horse was a long shot and no one at the shop, including myself, had ever heard of him. *Oh well! Maybe next year I'll pick a better horse,* I assured myself.

A little while later, I watched one of the best horse races I have ever seen in my entire life. "Oh my God! Thank you Jesus!" I shouted to the Lord. *What a wonderful blessing!* I thought. I watched in awe as one of the leading jockeys of all time led the horse "Ferdinand" around the race track straight to the winner's circle. Yes, the jockey had taken the horse for a ride of a lifetime. I couldn't believe it! The jockey led the winning horse through an unbelievable traffic. The jockey was a champ! The horse was a champ! I felt like a champ too, because, very unexpectedly, I was the proud winner of **"two Derby jackpots."**

Pregnant With Peeping Tom

If you've never seen a peeping Tom,
Don't look for him while on the john.

D.J. DeSai

It is a great blessing for me to know that I have God's protective shield around me twenty-four hours a day. I have to constantly remind myself, though, that he has promised to always be by my side, never to forsake me. During the event in this story, I had almost forgotten that the devil is my fear while the Lord is my refuge.

One day my husband Eric and I had been to his parents' home for a family reunion, and we didn't get back to our own house until around midnight. We both agreed we had a great time, although we had eaten far too many different kinds of foods that day. My stomach was taking the punishment for it, and I wasn't sure I would survive. I was feeling very sick.

I was almost eight months pregnant, so I was sure this had not helped matters when it came to my queasy tummy and all that I had eaten. My excuse was *I'm eating for two,* when it came to indulging the entire day. I allowed myself to try most of the different recipes that were brought to the reunion. My belly was telling me that I had made a huge mistake, but it was way too late to turn back now.

Eric, my husband, had just had a hernia operation a couple of days prior to the reunion, so he was not feeling well either. He was still very sore from the incision. Most of the day, he sat around in a Lazy Boy chair while his mother and I waited on him.

When the two of us got home that night, Eric did not waste any time heading to our bedroom. He immediately undressed, lay down, and turned on the television. I lay down beside him and tried to go to sleep, but I was feeling so nauseous that it was impossible for me to get comfortable. I got back up, deciding I must have a terrible case of indigestion.

I went to the bathroom, thinking I had to throw up. That procedure didn't seem to happen quickly enough, so I sat down on the toilet seat and just waited. One minute I thought I might vomit, while the next minute I wondered if I were going to have a bowel movement. I continued to sit there, feeling sicker by the moment. I had taken all my clothes off before I lay down with my husband, so all I had on was a housecoat and a big pair of granny underwear that barely covered my huge belly. As I sat there and stared at the gigantic round ball below me, I wondered if I were going to have twins. I had gained around thirty pounds already, and I was sure I could add on at least five more pounds from eating all the food at the reunion that day. I had only one more month to go before having my baby, so I had hoped I would not gain much more. "Ooh," I whispered to myself. "I'm feeling so sick."

All of a sudden, I started feeling very hot, as if I were breaking out with a fever. The bathroom window was open, and I could feel the cool breeze blowing in from outside, but it didn't seem to help me. I was also feeling woozy and clammy. I decided to take off my housecoat while sitting on the toilet seat for fear I would pass out from my heat spell. "Ooh, gee!" I whispered. *My stomach sickness has gotten worse,* I thought to myself. I reached over and splashed some cold water on my face, but that didn't seem to help much either. I grabbed the garbage can, feeling sure I would vomit soon.

As I sat there practically in the nude with nothing on but my great big underwear, I could do nothing but moan and groan. I wondered if I should wake Eric to tell him how awful I felt. I knew he didn't feel well either, and he was so worn out from the long day at the reunion. I decided to give myself a few more minutes to see if I would start feeling better. I was sure that all my symptoms had to be due to eating too much junk food. The thought did cross my mind that I may be going into labor, but I knew I still had one more miserable month left to go. I was so ready for my pregnancy to be over with.

While I sat there on the toilet seat, still holding on to the garbage can, I heard a noise that sounded like a tin can rattling right outside the bathroom window. I wondered if Eric had gotten up without my knowing about it. *Is he out in the back yard for some reason?* I wondered. *No,* I thought to myself. *He can't be. Eric is still walking slowly using a cane while healing from his hernia surgery. Besides, he's probably sound asleep by now,* I thought. *Oh well. The noise is probably coming from a stray dog or cat,* I assumed.

With a quick glance, I looked up at the opened bathroom window when all of a sudden I thought I would jump right out of my own skin. "Oh my God!" I shouted to the Lord. There was a peeping Tom looking through the screen of the bathroom window. He was staring a hole through me. He had the biggest, beadiest, scariest eyes I had ever seen in my whole life. He was not moving a muscle and both his eyes were fixed right on me.

As I sat there on the toilet seat, all I could manage to do was scream the loudest scream I had ever heard come out of my own mouth. I had no idea that there could be that much noise stored inside my voice box. I quickly grabbed the shower curtain and pulled it over the top of me to hide my pregnant and almost naked body. At the same time, it seemed like our eyes had locked for the longest time, but I was sure it was only for a few short seconds.

All the while I continued to cry out for help as loudly as I could. Sitting there feeling more than frightened, I heard Eric jump up from the bed while yelling out my name. "Dory, what's wrong?" Eric shouted. All I really remember is how I couldn't stop screaming. I was sure that my husband had made it to the bathroom very quickly, but each moment seemed like an eternity.

When Eric barged through the door, I just sat there pointing at the bathroom window. I somehow managed to tell him that there was someone out there. I didn't know if I was making sense to him or not. Thank God, he knew what I was saying. Eric waved his cane in his hand, pointed it to the window and told me he'd be right back. I heard him say that whoever was out there would be sorry after he got hold of him and beat the heck out of him. I assumed Eric would beat the peeping Tom up with his cane, but I was worried because I was sure my husband's incision had not healed enough for him to fight someone. He was still hobbling around, hardly able to walk. I knew I had to go check on him and call the police.

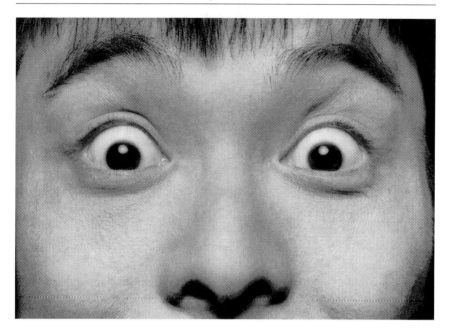

When I was finally able to get up from the toilet seat, I walked into the hallway. Needless to say, my stomach was feeling so nervous, but my nausea had finally subsided. Now, I was in shock. I was probably too scared to be sick. *How could anyone be so cruel to a woman carrying a child?* I wondered. What bothered me more than anything was that the peeping Tom had seen me sitting on the toilet seat with no clothes on. I was so disturbed by this that when Eric came back into the house, I was standing there crying my eyes out. He reached out and hugged me, and told me everything would be okay. I finally settled down some. I thanked Eric and then I thanked the Lord. I was so grateful for their help.

Eric went into the bathroom to close and lock the window. Then he pulled the curtain closed so no one could see in. "There is no way that anyone could have seen you while looking in the bathroom window without standing on something outside," Eric told me. "The window is too high," he said. I told my husband about the noise I had heard earlier and that I had just assumed it was a stray animal at first. He just shook his head with an aggravated look. He was very upset, too.

I thanked Eric again for chasing away the peeping Tom, and asked him what had taken place outside. He said nothing had happened, because the guy had jumped the fence and gotten away before he was able to get close to him. *Maybe that was for the best,* I thought. *After all, Eric is still healing from his hernia surgery,* I reminded myself.

After the two of us had regained our composure, Eric called the police and made a report. The policemen said there had been several calls made that week regarding the same incident in the neighborhood. "Gee! It sure would have been nice to have known this," I told them. They assured me and Eric that the man had not broken into anyone's home or hurt anyone. They said he was a harmless peeping Tom. "Just a harmless peeping Tom," I repeated sarcastically. "Wow! I still feel violated," I told the policemen. "Even though I may have frightened him as much as he had me, it was wrong," I told them. Everyone laughed at my comment, including Eric.

As I stood there feeling upset, I didn't know if I should laugh or cry. The policemen acted as though the incident was not a big deal, but Eric and I surely thought it was. For me, the entire episode was a huge nightmare. It was also a miracle that I hadn't had a miscarriage that night. *Oh, man!* I kept thinking. *I'll never forget those big, scary, beady eyes staring a hole through me. What a picture, and it will always haunt my mind.* Imagine a woman sitting on the toilet seat, practically in the nude, hugging the garbage can feeling nothing but sick to her stomach while **"pregnant with peeping Tom."**

Heartbreaking Break-In

Thou shall not steal; the Bible tells us so,
It's heartless, it's cold, and a big no, no.

D.J. DeSai

Several years ago, I started receiving several hang-up calls at my home during all hours of the day and night. These calls persisted on a regular basis for at least a couple of weeks. I just assumed that people were dialing the wrong number and then hanging up, but I wondered why all of a sudden the calls kept occurring so much more than usual. I never really thought about it much then, but I most certainly do now. This is why.

While working my part-time job from ten o'clock in the morning until three in the afternoon, I spent most late afternoons and nights at home with my two children. My husband, Barry, worked a night job. His working hours were from four o'clock in the afternoon until twelve midnight. Oftentimes, it would be one or two in the morning before he would arrive home.

Occasionally, I would go out with some of my girlfriends and listen to different bands play music just to pass the time away while waiting for Barry to come home. I have always loved music because I grew up listening to my dad and his bluegrass band play once or twice a week.

One afternoon a girlfriend of mine named Gina called and asked me to go out and listen to one of her favorite bands that would be in town for only that night. I was so thrilled that she had asked me to go. I loved the band, as Gina did. While thinking about the time frame that Gina said they would be playing music, I almost backed out of going. I told her it was too late for us to be out in a nightclub. Gina agreed, but she told me the gig would be superb. I couldn't argue with her on that note, so I told her I would think about going and let her know what my decision was later that afternoon.

After I hung the phone up with Gina, I called Barry and told him that my girlfriend had called and asked me to go out. I explained to him that it would be late when I got home if I decided to go. Barry told me I should go on out and listen to the band with Gina. He told me I deserved to get out of the house and if I didn't make it back home before he did, he would wait up for me. He also told me to call his mom to ask her to watch the kids, since she had suggested babysitting a few nights prior. I thought about it for a few minutes and then called Barry's mom to see if the kids could spend the night with her. Of course, my mother-in-law sounded anxious to see her grandbabies. She told me she would even stop by to pick them up later that afternoon. I thanked her as I hung the phone up. Then I called Gina back to tell her I would go. We both couldn't wait to hear the band. We were so excited.

The two of us made plans to meet each other at a certain time in the parking lot of the nightclub so we would not have to walk in alone. The location where we were going had a high crime rate, so we did not want to take any chances. After we came to a mutual agreement on our meeting, we hung the phones up.

Around seven-thirty that night, I started getting ready. I showered, put my make-up on, and got dressed. I carefully chose my costume jewelry to match my out-fit. I decided not to wear anything of excessive value because of where we were going that night. Again, it was not the better part of town. I didn't want to attract any kind of attention to myself, so I dressed as inexpensive as I could.

My mom had recently given me her first engagement ring that my dad had given to her before they had gotten married. I was so proud to wear my mom's ring on my finger. It was a little too big for me, but I had not had the chance to get it resized. I took the ring off my finger, and placed it safely in my jewelry box. I did not want to lose something that was so sentimental to me and my mother, and theft had also crossed my mind.

Nine o'clock came late that night. It was finally time for me to leave my house to go meet Gina. The band was to start playing at ten o'clock, and they were scheduled to finish their gig around two in the morning. Gina had told me they were charging a fairly steep cover to get inside to see the show, so the two of us decided we would stay until it was over. We told each other that if we were not too tired, we would stay until they played the very last song, and we did.

When we left the club that night to head home, we hugged each other and promised not to wait so long to get together again. We both had a great time, and the band could not have sounded any better. We were so happy we had decided to go.

It was around two-thirty in the morning when I finally arrived home. Anxiously, my heart skipped several beats as I drove my car slowly down the dead-end street while staring at a flashing blue police light that was directly in front of mine and Barry's house. I pulled into our driveway to find the front door wide open, with Barry and two police officers standing inside talking. *What in the world is going on?* I wondered. I jumped out of my car and quickly ran inside. "What happened?" I asked Barry. With a very distraught look on his face, Barry told me that our home had been broken into just a few minutes prior. "Oh no!" I cried. Barry said, "Calm down, Dory. We'll get through this." He put his arm around me while telling me that he had come home from work and caught the burglars in the act. He said they had rushed out the basement door, darted through the back yard, and then jumped the fence. Barry said he had tried to catch them but he couldn't. He immediately called the police. He said the officers had just arrived right before I had gotten home.

Both Barry and I stood in our living room in shock, as the police officers made a report. I walked up the steps of our bi-level home to find nothing but a complete mess to clean up. The burglars, who Barry said were four teenagers, had ransacked our entire house. They had broken a piggy bank that belonged to our son, Jake. It had several sentimental coins inside it. Of course, the money was gone. They had taken every piece of my undergarments out of every drawer in the dresser and chest of drawers. Every piece of clothing was just lying on the bed and the floor.

Feeling an overwhelming sickness penetrate deep inside the pit of my belly as I visualized the burglars touching everything I owned, I ran to the restroom. All I could do was cry, feeling my heart breaking in two. *How could they do something like this to someone else's belongings?* I wondered. *I do not understand.* "Oh my God!" I cried out to the Lord, as I looked down at my jewelry box lying on the floor empty. My mother's first engagement ring and every other piece of jewelry I treasured were gone. I quickly found my keepsake box that had been lying on my dresser and opened it up. This was the place I had kept my grandfather's silver dollars that he had given to me so many years ago. They were all gone, too. I felt overwhelmed. I had never before felt so empty and hurt inside. My heart was aching so badly.

All of a sudden I felt fear starting to set in while I wondered if the burglars would come back again. *How can we stay in this house?* I asked myself. The police officers must have known how I was feeling because one of them sympathetically reached out and touched my arm to comfort me. He told me they were sorry, and then asked me if I had noticed anything out of the ordinary lately. I told them no. Suddenly I remembered the hang-up phone calls I had received the past several nights. I told the police officers about them. They said the robbery was probably planned, and the teenagers were just waiting for the right time to break in. They had waited until Barry went to work and I had left the house before they broke in.

Wishing with all of my whole heart that I had stayed home that night, I stood there and cried again. The police officers tried to console me, but it wasn't working. They told me this had happened a lot lately in the neighborhood, and they were looking for the burglars. They also told me if I could remember anything else to give them a call, as one officer handed me his business card. Before they left, they told me and Barry to assess our losses before calling the insurance company for reimbursement.

Barry cleaned up most of the mess and changed the sheets and spreads on our bed. I was still not able to get myself together completely. I kept breaking down every time I noticed something sentimental missing. *I'm nothing but a mess, but who wouldn't be?* I told myself. *Strangers have broken into our home and touched or stolen almost everything we own.*

Barry and I managed to go to bed that night, but neither one of us were able to sleep for very long. I kept thinking about the robbers coming back, and everything that they had stolen. It had truly damaged me emotionally and mentally. Barry wondered if and when I would eventually settle down, as he worried about our missing belongings, too. He didn't know what to say or do to make me feel any better. Most everything with sentimental value had belonged to me. Barry was only missing the television set, the stereo, and the music tapes. These things could all be replaced with the insurance money.

The next day after the two of us cleaned the house thoroughly again, we sat down together and made a list of everything we were missing and the value of it all. We knew we had to contact our insurance company so we could be compensated for our losses. I was still sick from being so upset. My fear of the burglars coming back was starting to turn into hurt now. I felt as though I had lost my best friend, because losing all of my material things that meant so much to me had really hit me hard. I remembered two cameo rings that my dad had given to me. They were so sentimental, not to mention my mom's first engagement ring I had just taken off my finger that night for fear of losing it or having it stolen.

My grandfather had been killed on a tractor at a very early age, and the silver dollars that were stolen were all I had left from him. Someone had just offered me two hundred dollars for one of my old silver coins. I had firmly said "no way" to the huge offer, because it meant so much to me. Now, I had nothing left.

Thankfully, it didn't take long for my hurt feelings to turn into angry feelings. All of a sudden I was wishing the robbers would walk back through the door one more time. I would be ready for them this time. Although I did not own a gun, I was so mad that I thought I could whip them all with my bare hands.

Every time I would leave the house, I only hoped and prayed the robbers would be there when I returned home. My anger would not bring my stuff back, but it sure helped me to cope. I knew my grandfather would not want me to get all bogged down with my losses and I was trying not to, but it wasn't easy. My grandfather was a very godly man and he had always told me to never store my treasures on this earth, but instead, to store them in heaven. What he meant by this statement was to never put any great emphasis on material things, because we cannot take them with us when we leave this world. I knew this thought was true wisdom from above, but deep down inside I still wanted my belongings back. They were mine.

I started searching the pawn shops every chance I had, hoping I would find something that belonged to me. If this were to happen, hopefully, I could buy it back, but I had no luck. Sad to say, I also found out that I did not have an additional jewelry insurance policy, so I was not even able to collect money on most of what I had lost. My daddy was right. He had always told me that life is not fair, and now I could surely relate to that.

I started saying prayers, asking Jesus to help me get over what had happened to me and Barry that night. I told the Lord I did not want to hold nor harbor any bad feelings inside me against anyone else. I knew it would only hurt me in the end. I even prayed for the burglars, asking God to bless them and to help them to understand they were hurting other people. I prayed that Jesus would convict them of their sin so that they would stop robbing people. I also prayed for their repentance of their sins and their salvation. These prayers had made me feel better, so I was sure I was on my way to forgiving and also forgetting the horrible **"heartbreaking break-in."**

The Size of a Snake

Big or little, short or tall,
You're the one who makes the call.

D.J. DeSai

People come in different sizes, shapes, and colors. No one is alike. We all have different ideas, too, and form our own opinions about everything. I say this makes life exciting. Imagine a world of people where everyone is identical. How boring! We might as well be robots.

From the day I was born until I turned twelve years old, my family and I lived in Kentucky outside the city of Lawrenceburg. The country land that surrounded our home was filled with all kinds of small and large animals. I would play outside nearly every day, feeling little or no fear of anything, probably because I did not know any better. My mother, Leola, knew about being afraid though, and she always tried to protect her children from harm, as any good parent would do.

I remember my mom grabbing a garden hoe almost every day and using it to cut the heads off of snakes. This was just a normal procedure for her, and I almost felt sorry for the creepy looking beings. Mom hated snakes, and she was afraid of them, and she also feared that they may hurt her children. She would run and get the garden hoe as soon as she laid eyes on one. Yes, she had become a "pro with her hoe," so to speak, when it came to killing snakes.

One summer day I was playing in the back yard when an approximately two to three feet long snake fell out of a tree and onto my shoulders. It wasn't a light-weighted snake either, as it fell onto my less than one hundred pound body. I felt the moist, heavy, slimy, snaky sensation all over my neck, shoulders, and arms. I quickly shrugged it off of me before it had time to hug my neck.

Over the years, I have often wondered if the incident were an accident on the snake's part or if the snake had aimed to fall on me. It didn't really matter much anyway because I wasn't afraid of it. Why should I be? It wasn't one of the largest snakes I had seen before, and I had never been bitten or hurt by one. Knowing how my mom felt about them though, I was definitely not going to take the time to befriend one of them either. I never did tell anyone about the snake falling on me that day, because I did not want to see the reptile get beheaded, especially for no good reason. That one particular snake survived Mom and was able to live a little longer because of me not telling about it. I didn't really like snakes, but I didn't dislike them either. I did hate seeing them lose their life with my mom's hoe, but I was sure it was the right thing for her to do.

Several years later, my parents moved the entire family to the big city. After graduating from high school, I met a young man named Barry. We dated for several months and then married. Soon afterwards, we bought a home and started a family. Sad to say, a few years later our marriage ended in divorce.

One summer day, though, while Barry and I were still married, he was out in the back yard cutting the grass. Suddenly, I saw him barge through the back door as if a monster were chasing him down. In no time at all, I saw my husband dash into the garage, looking as white as a ghost and screaming something about seeing a snake in the back yard. Then I heard him say he thought he had run over it with the lawn mower. "Oh my God!" I shouted, praying that Barry was okay. He was moving so fast that I couldn't tell.

Suddenly, I became so excited! I couldn't believe it! I had not seen a snake since my family and I had moved from the country to the city. I quickly rushed out the back door into the yard where the lawn mower was sitting. I could hear Barry yelling at me in the background, pleading with me to stop because the snake may still be alive. "Wait, Dory. Don't go near the lawn mower," Barry shouted. I was so thrilled to think that I might be able to capture a small bit of my country roots again by viewing the live snake. Naturally, I refused to listen to my husband's words of concern. I couldn't wait to see the big snake!

When I approached the lawn mower I immediately looked on the ground directly in front of it. From a distance, I saw nothing. As I got closer, I saw what appeared to be a large worm that was barely able to move. It was lying in the grass. *Yes, Barry has definitely hit it with the lawn mower,* I thought. When I stooped down and got a closer look, I was sure it was a baby garden snake instead of a worm. Suddenly, I started laughing so hard that I almost wet my pants before I made it back to the house. I could not believe Barry was so freaked out and scared over something as small as a little bitty baby snake. *Poor guy,* I thought. *I wonder if he has ever met up with a full grown snake before.*

After I walked back in the house, I saw Barry just standing there with a solemn look on his face. I was still laughing uncontrollably. I was sure I must have hurt his feelings by laughing out loud, but I couldn't help it. I could not understand his frantic reaction to the little snake. I was also sure he did not comprehend how I was feeling either because he had never experienced a taste of the country life as I had. If Barry had seen what I have always called a big snake, he may have had a heart attack and died right there on the spot just like the little, mutilated snake that he had run over with the lawn mower.

Needless to say, this experience made a very fond memory for me. I only hope Barry can laugh about it now, too. If nothing else, I believe he will be quick to say that the size of a snake is irrelevant, and is surely in the eye of the beholder. Of course, now, I agree. I say if you ever run into this scaly, slippery, and oftentimes dangerous being, keep your eye on it. It may make no difference to you at all when it comes to **"the size of a snake."**

Stone Crazy

You may be called a little dense,
If you are lacking common sense.

D.J. DeSai

If we are learning something every day, I believe we are growing, and this is all that matters in our spiritual walk. I am sure that no one in this world knows everything there is to know, except for our God. Isn't the earth a wonderful place the Lord has created for us? I say we are being prepared for heaven while we're here, so that when we die we can move on and reside with so much more intellect. I am looking forward to a perfected world called heaven where we can reign with Jesus Christ. I believe it will be a place where there will be no pain, no tears, and a beautiful life that will last forever. Praise Jesus!

I feel the need to share another story that my friend Jody revealed to me several years ago. She described to me in detail another personal and shocking dilemma that she was given no choice but to endure. I hope you will benefit from reading this story, and enjoy it, too.

My friend Jody woke up one morning feeling good. She got ready and drove the five minute drive to get to her workplace. After two hours of filing forms and taking inventory, Jody started feeling some low back pain and stomach cramps. She thought maybe she had pulled a muscle so she assumed the pain would eventually go away, but it gradually worsened as the day slowly passed. By three o'clock that afternoon she began hurting so badly that she was bent completely over with pain. She was barely able to walk by then.

Jody couldn't wait to get home that afternoon so she could lie down. She thought she would feel better once she took a couple of aspirins and rested for a few minutes. She wondered if it were time for her monthly period. She was feeling so much pain, unlike anything else she had ever felt before, with the exception of labor pains. Believing she was blessed just to make it home that day, Jody quickly got out of her car, ran into the house, and jumped in her bed. That was just about all the strength she had left from all the pain she was enduring.

Shortly thereafter, her husband Harry came up from the basement and found her lying on the bed moaning and groaning. She told him how she had been feeling all day. She also told him that if he didn't do something soon, she felt as though she might die. Harry felt sorry for Jody and was very worried about her. He asked her what she wanted him to do. She told him she needed something stronger than the aspirin she had already taken. He told her he would drive to the nearby drugstore to pick something else up for her. Jody told Harry what her symptoms were. She told him that she was experiencing excruciating cramping in her lower back and abdomen, and she was hurting as much as--if not more than--she had while giving birth to their children. Thank God, their two children had stayed over at a friend's house that day after school. Jody didn't think she was capable of taking care of them while feeling so badly.

After Harry left for the drugstore, Jody forced herself to get up and walk to the bathroom. She wondered if she would make it and thought she would fall to the floor because the pain was so intense by then. She also wondered if she were having a miscarriage, although she felt sure it had not been long since she had her last period. Finally, she was able to turn the bathroom light on while holding on to the sink for support. Then she sat down on the toilet seat. "Oh my God!" Jody cried out to Jesus. "Help me Lord!" All she could do was pray. She was sure her cramps could not get any worse.

Feeling terrified for her life, she sat there for a few minutes before deciding she'd better try to make it to the kitchen so she could call 911. When she got up, she immediately fell right back down on the commode. As she sat there filled with fear, thinking she may very well be near her death, she wondered how much longer she could survive.

Suddenly, Jody heard a small noise. What she had heard was the sound of something that had fallen and hit the water inside the toilet bowl. She also felt relief concerning the pain in her stomach and lower back after this had happened. When Jody was finally able to stand up, she looked inside the commode and saw a small but somewhat round and jagged stone. She reached her hand inside the toilet bowl, and picked it up from the water. She was carefully examining it when she heard Harry walk in the front door.

While Jody's pain had almost subsided, she saw Harry place his hand inside a plastic grocery bag. He handed her a bottle of pills that he had picked up at the drugstore. The pills were for menstrual cramps. Jody couldn't help but smile because she knew Harry was only trying to help her. She felt so glad to be alive after what she had just been through. She realized she should have gone to the hospital, but her pain was so horrific at the time that she didn't even know what she needed. Maybe Harry should have known, though, but they were both very young.

Jody explained to Harry what had happened while he was gone. She told him she had somehow made it to the bathroom. She showed him the tiny stone that was still in the palm of her hand. She explained to him how the stone had fallen into the toilet. Then she told him how sore her stomach was, although the excruciating pain she had felt was gone. She went on to tell him that she had passed a kidney stone, and she was sure she should have gone to the hospital immediately after work. She felt silly! "Who would think that a twenty-five year old woman could have a kidney stone?" Jody asked me. "I never would have thought that. Who would have thought I could have passed it on my own? I wonder how I did it. It sure wasn't easy," Jody says.

Harry disagreed with Jody, telling her he didn't think that what she was holding in her hand was a kidney stone. He told her she must have swallowed a shell while they were in Florida vacationing a few weeks prior. *Oh my!* Jody thought, as she stood there dumbfounded. She waited for Harry to start laughing, but he didn't. She couldn't believe what he had said. That was the craziest thing she had ever heard. Jody loved her husband, but she thought he must have been out of his head for making that statement to her, and she told him so. Jody still believes Harry had to be teasing with her, but he never owned up to it.

A few years later she and Harry divorced, although their break-up had nothing to do with stones or shells. To this day, though, Jody says if Harry still believes she swallowed a shell instead of passing a kidney stone, then not only does she think he's still crazy, she thinks he's **"stone crazy."**

Two Dollars and One Ticket

Keep your treasure close to you,
And don't take it for granted, whatever you do.

D.J. DeSai

"You don't know what you've got till it's gone," has always been one of my favorite sayings. Looking back on some of my past experiences, I truly believe these famous words have taught me a few lessons. What's really amazing is that oftentimes one incident can illustrate more than one lesson taught, as in this story.

I grew up around race horses; therefore, I couldn't help but take an interest in them every once in a while. I'd never been one to gamble a lot of money on a horse race, but sometimes I'd bet a small amount of money on a long shot, and take a chance on winning more. I'd also lose that small amount of money sometimes, too.

Many horse race tracks offer a special bet called the pick-six. This means if you pick the winners of all six races, you win the amount of money that that bet pays off. If no one picks all six races correctly, most of the money stays in the pot, and it keeps growing until someone does win it. A small amount of that money is usually paid out to the winners of five races.

One day Judy, a very good friend of mine, called to ask me if I were going to the race track that same night. Judy told me the pick-six carry-over amount had totaled fifty thousand dollars, and she asked me if I would place a bet for her if I were going. I told Judy I didn't know if I would go or not, but I would call her later to let her know for sure.

When I got home from work that night, I had an itching to go somewhere, so I figured the race track would be as good a place as any. I called Judy, wrote down the bet she wanted, dressed myself, and then helped my daughter Mindy get dressed. We were ready to go.

Mindy, my six-year-old daughter, loved going to the race track because she loved eating the junk food they sold there. I didn't have to twist her arm to persuade her to go, because she knew I would buy her some kind of treat before we left the track. Of course, she had to behave if she were to get one. On the other hand, my son Jake was the complete opposite. When I asked him if he wanted to go, he said no. He asked me if he could stay with his friend who lived down the street. He wanted to play video games with him. I told him yes, that I would drop him off there and pick him back up on my way home. I told Jake that Mindy and I would be gone for only a couple of hours.

It was crowded that night at the track, because the pick-six carry over had climbed so high. I was guessing that everyone wanted to try his luck at picking the six winners, and I was excited about it, too. I sat down on the bench with Mindy, my cute little six-year old blonde-haired beauty, while I wrote down my pick-six bet. I didn't have a lot of time to spare before the first race of the pick-six, and the betting line had gotten very long. I knew I would have to hurry if I were to get mine and Judy's bets.

Mindy and I stood in line for about fifteen minutes before I was finally able to purchase our tickets. I put the tickets safely in my purse, feeling relieved to get that part over with. I decided to stay for only a couple of races before heading home. I knew that we would all have to get up early the next morning, so I didn't want to stay out too late.

After the two races were over and Mindy and I were headed for the exit door, we ran into Alex, a friend of mine. I stopped to talk with Alex just long enough for him to tell me that I might want to bet the last race of the night. Alex said the pool money for this race was estimated to be almost four thousand dollars. He told me that I should purchase a ticket for that race before I left the track. I thanked him and told him I might just do that on my way out.

After Alex and I said goodbye, I reached in my purse and pulled out two one-dollar bills. I decided I would go ahead and get a two-dollar straight bet on the superfecta race that Alex had told me about. This meant I had to pick the first four horses in order; each horse had to come in first, second, third, and fourth if I were to win. It was probably an impossible bet to win, but I decided to buy a ticket anyway, since I was standing so close to the betting window. After all, it was a small bet and a chance to win big.

I turned around and laid my two dollars on the counter. Then I told the cashier I wanted a superfecta bet on the last race, as I recited the four numbers to him. I told him I wanted the numbers four, three, eight, and one. I figured I had just as good a chance picking my bet this way as studying the racing form, which I did not have the time to do anyway. The cashier handed me my ticket, and I turned around to tell Mindy it was time for us to go home. Suddenly, I panicked! Mindy was not there! She had been right beside me all night long. Now she had disappeared in what seemed like only a couple of seconds. *Where in the world is she?* I wondered.

Anxiously, my eyes started searching all over the place as fast as they could possibly move. All I could see were too many faces and so many bodies, but none of them was Mindy's. I quickly felt terror! I started running as fast as I could. Finally, I made it to the exit door, thinking that maybe Mindy had started walking toward it, since that was where we were headed before I decided to buy the last ticket. Mindy knew the two of us were almost ready to leave, so maybe she had kept walking that way. Oh! How I was praying my daughter would be standing by the exit door waiting for me.

Trying my best to remain calm, I started remembering back, longing to think of the very last moment I had seen my daughter. I knew Mindy was standing right next to me while I was talking with my friend Alex. That was right before I had bought the last two-dollar ticket. *Where could Mindy have taken off to so quickly?* I kept asking myself.

Suddenly, I became more than frightened! I started remembering a report the local television news had been broadcasting the past couple of nights. They had been warning people of a series of kidnappings going on in the city, and it appeared they had all been linked to blonde-haired, blue-eyed little girls around the same age as Mindy.

Naturally, I started feeling so sick inside the pit of my stomach. I also started shaking all over as I ran up to the security guard standing by the exit door. I asked him if he had seen my little girl, and I started explaining to him what Mindy was wearing and what she looked like. The security guard told me he thought he had seen her leave the building a short while ago. "Oh my God!" I prayed, as I ran out the door as fast as I could. If I could just find Mindy, I promised myself I would never take her to a place like this again. I started pleading with the Lord to bring my daughter back to me. I ran all over the parking lot, but I did not see her anywhere. The security guard was helping me look for Mindy, too. The two of us were anything but calm.

Outside, it was so dark and quiet that I could have heard a pin drop. There was no sign of my child anywhere in sight. I started screaming Mindy's name as loudly as I could, but still, there was no sound. I was so hyped-up that I wondered if I might pass out right there in the parking lot. I was definitely having an anxiety attack.

Frantically, I ran back inside the building again but still, I could not find her. I was devastated! I felt as though my spirit had died, as I stood there feeling so helpless. I also felt like I had lost my own life. *Without Mindy, I can not and will not live,* I thought to myself. *My children mean everything to me.* I knew this was my own fault. I had been so busy worrying about my stupid bet and silly ticket that I had not watched over my daughter closely enough. I was surely blaming myself. The thought of a horse race was making me feel sicker than I already was, as I continued to panic.

My eyes were still searching a mile a minute when suddenly, and thank God, I caught a glimpse of Mindy standing by the concession stand in front of a long line of people. "Yes!" I gasped. *There stands my sweet Mindy, and what a beautiful sight she is,* I thought to myself as I thanked God. I decided right then and there that I would never take my eyes off my daughter again. I watched as my blonde-haired beauty just stood there looking content, watching people eat their junk food. Suddenly, I remembered I had promised Mindy a treat before we left the race track if she were a good girl. She had not forgotten about it, but I most certainly had.

Breathing a huge sigh of relief, I began to calm down. Then I broke down and cried, knowing I probably shouldn't let Mindy see my tears. I felt like hugging and spanking her all at the same time. I did not want to scare her, because she looked so innocent just standing there, but I had to let my daughter know that she shouldn't walk off from me again. I also wanted to make sure that she knew to go to a security officer if she ever got lost.

Hastily, I rushed over and grabbed Mindy. I held my little girl so tightly in my arms. I wasn't even sure she knew she was lost, because she was simply watching the waiter serve cotton candy and popcorn. She looked as though she did not have a care in the world and was having the time of her life doing nothing but watch the food leave one hand and go to another. My little girl loved treats, and I was so happy to see her that I told her she could have anything she wanted at the concession stand. Mindy hugged, kissed, and thanked me for her cotton candy as we walked to the car and headed for home.

I was so happy to get away from the race track. It would be a long time before I cared to go back again and even longer than that if I had my children with me. I praised Jesus for keeping Mindy safe. I went to bed that night, so thankful to have both my kids tucked securely in their beds. I thought about all the parents who had lost their children to kidnappings, so I said a prayer for them before I fell to sleep.

The next morning after I had gotten ready to go to work, I picked up the newspaper to see if my pick-six tickets were any good. No, I had not won, and Judy hadn't either. I didn't even mind much that I had lost, because I had found Mindy, and I was still so thankful for it. I praised Jesus again for my blessings!

On my way to work that morning, I suddenly remembered I had purchased the two-dollar superfecta ticket right before I lost Mindy. I had almost forgotten about the ticket because of all the commotion. It was something that I really didn't care to recall, although I had been taught a lesson. I would not take my children's safety for granted in a crowded place again. I would always watch them more closely from this day forward.

I picked up the newspaper when I got to work to see what the winning numbers were for the superfecta race I had bet on. The numbers that had come in were four, three, eight, and one. "Oh my goodness!" I shouted. I had won the four thousand dollars that had been carried over for that race. I started jumping up and down with joy, telling everyone at my workplace that I had won the money. My co-workers were very happy for me as they congratulated me. Gee! I was ecstatic! I could surely use the extra money. *Wow! What had previously seemed like an awful night has taken a one hundred eighty-degree turn,* I thought to myself. *I am a rich woman now. I've won four thousand dollars.* "Yippee!" I shouted.

When I opened my purse to look for the ticket I had purchased, it was not there. The pick-six tickets were tucked inside a compartment, but the two-dollar superfecta ticket was missing. I must have taken it out of my purse, so I was certain it was somewhere at home. Suddenly, I remembered putting the ticket inside my shirt pocket right before I lost Mindy. *Yes! The winning ticket is inside my shirt pocket,* I thought to myself. *I'm sure it is.* I was positively hoping it was, anyway.

Around lunch time, I asked my boss if I could run home to look for my ticket, because it was driving me crazy not having it with me. After all, it was worth four thousand dollars. My boss told me it was okay for me to go, so I rushed out the door to go find my treasure.

After I pulled into the driveway, I jumped out of the car and ran into the house. The first thing I did was look for my clothing I had worn the night before. Thinking I knew exactly where my winning ticket was, I quickly looked inside the pocket of my shirt. *Oh no! It's not here. I must have put it in my jeans pocket,* I thought to myself. I hurriedly picked up my pants and searched all the pockets. The ticket was not there either. I was starting to feel very anxious. *I'm certain I put the four-thousand dollar ticket in my shirt pocket, but where in the world is it?* I wondered. I searched the shirt pocket again and again. I felt as though I was having another panic attack like I had the night before when I lost Mindy. I knew I had put the ticket somewhere, but I did not have the time to keep searching for it. I needed to get back to work because it was getting late. I told myself I would find the ticket later when I had more time.

I drove back to my workplace, and as soon as I walked in the door, everyone was quick to ask me if I had found my ticket. My co-workers were as concerned about the ticket as I was. I told them no, but I knew I would find it later. I told them I wasn't worried about it, although deep down inside, I was very concerned. I wondered if I had lost the ticket in the midst of thinking I had lost Mindy. I felt as though I was starting to lose my mind too, not being able to find the winning four-thousand dollar ticket. I probably just needed to rest. I was feeling so stressed and tired.

That night I went home and hunted all over the place again. I looked in all the same spots I had already looked. Not only did I look once, I looked two, three, four, and five times but still, no ticket was to be found. I kept thinking I was just overlooking it, and that I would eventually find it. I searched my car thoroughly, and everywhere else I could think of. There just didn't seem to be a ticket anywhere in sight, and I was getting so discouraged. I knew the most important of anything that night was finding Mindy, but four thousand dollars was a tremendous amount of money to lose. I wanted it so badly.

I had always made it a habit of checking my numbers to make sure they were correct immediately after purchasing a ticket at the track. I remembered checking the ticket afterwards and again, I was certain I had put it in my shirt pocket. I did not remember putting it anywhere else. Maybe I had dropped the ticket on the floor at the race track. No matter, I could not give up looking for it. Surely I would eventually find it. *I could not have lost four thousand dollars,* I told myself. I continued to get very aggravated about the entire ordeal, but I still couldn't let it go. *It is way too much money and I want it. I need it. I have to have it,* I kept thinking.

During the next few days, I continued to search for the missing winning ticket, although I started thinking it was just not meant to be for me to find it. Maybe the Lord was trying to tell me something. Maybe he wanted to teach me some things. I had found Mindy that night, and that was a huge blessing. Of course, no amount of money in the whole wide world could buy or replace one of my children, so maybe I was just being selfish for wanting the ticket so badly. No matter, I had become so obsessed looking for it. I couldn't help it. It was my money, but only if I could find the ticket.

I called and talked with one of the race track attendants a few days later to ask him if the ticket had been cashed yet. He told me, no. No one had come forth with the winning ticket as of yet, he said. I told him my sad story, but it did not seem to matter to him or anyone else who worked there. The attendants needed my ticket to pay me the money I had won. They told me this was their policy, and I understood. They also told me if the ticket had gotten swept up with the garbage at the race track, it was long gone by now. They went on to say that they were very sorry.

A few days later, I made a huge mistake of telling one of my regular clients, Ed, about my lost daughter and lost ticket story. Ed couldn't believe it either. He owned a little store next to my workplace. After I told my story to him, every day when I would walk to the bank, he would yell at me and ask me if I had found my ticket yet. Every day I would tell him no, I had not found it. Ed's obsession with my lost ticket was getting so depressing for me. *Why can't he just forget about it?* I wondered. I did not want to hear about the stupid ticket anymore because, finally, I had almost given up on the thought of ever finding it. Just thinking about all the lost money was frustrating enough for me. I surely didn't need to be reminded of it every single day of my life. I only wished now that I had never told Ed or anyone else about it.

I started walking on the opposite side of the street every day when I would go to the bank, just to avoid Ed. By doing this, I wouldn't have to listen to his "lost ticket" comments. *Ed is a nice man, but enough is enough already,* I thought. *He should know he's bringing up a bad memory for me. He should also know I just want to forget about the lost ticket. Can't he put himself in my shoes? I only wish he would,* I told myself.

The next few days I had the pleasure of not seeing Ed, so I guessed he was in the back of his store working. As long as I did not have to hear about my lost ticket, I did not really care what he was doing. I only needed a break from all his comments and the negativity that had haunted me for the last several weeks.

One day, while I was on my way to the bank and as I was crossing the street, I heard Ed yelling for me to come over to where he was. At first I just ignored him. "Dory, I need to talk to you," Ed shouted to me again. I wondered what in the world he would have to say now. Couldn't he tell I was trying to avoid him? I guessed not, because he sure was trying to get my attention. I went ahead and headed in his direction to see what he wanted. I figured I'd let him verbally abuse me one last time, but this would be it. I would tell him today that I did not want to hear one more comment concerning my lost ticket. I was more than tired of it. It was high time now to let him know this, too.

I walked over to where Ed was when I instantly noticed he had a very disturbed look on his face. I asked him if there was something wrong. He told me yes and asked me if I knew he had been on vacation the previous week. I told him that I had not seen him for awhile and wondered where he was. I didn't want to tell him that I had been very thankful not to see him because of his comments about my lost ticket.

Ed went on to tell me about a trip he had taken to Las Vegas the week before. He told me that he had saved up five thousand dollars of his earned money to take with him on his gambling trip. He went on to tell me that he had never made it out of the Vegas airport with his money. I asked him why. Ed said that he had been pick-pocketed at the airport the day he arrived in Las Vegas, and that someone had taken all five thousand dollars of his hard earned money. I couldn't believe it. "Who could have done that without your knowing about it?" I asked him. Ed said that the policemen in Las Vegas had told him that pick-pocketing had been reported numerous times lately, and he never should have put his money inside his pocket like that, especially in a public place such as an airport.

Ed proceeded to tell me that what had happened to him was way worse than what had happened to me because all I had really lost was two dollars of my money while he had lost all five thousand dollars of his. He went on to explain to me that I could not count the four thousand dollars as money I had lost because I never had the money to begin with. He, on the other hand, had lost his money that he had worked very hard for. I just stared at him while feeling a loss for words, although I understood what he was saying to me.

Sincerely, Ed promised me that he would never bring up my lost ticket again if I would never mention his five thousand dollars that someone had pick-pocketed from him. He was so sick about his stolen money, and this had made him realize that I must still be sick, too, over my lost ticket. I told him that I loved his idea very much. I also told him that I was sure we would both be better off to just forget about all of it. There was nothing that either one of us could do about our losses anyway. He agreed.

Ed must have had his entire vacation week to think about my lost ticket and his stolen money. I had guessed he had nothing else to do that week but to think, since he had no money to gamble while he vacationed in Las Vegas. I actually felt sorry for Ed so before I left him, I reached over and gave him a big hug and told him I was so sorry about what had happened to him, and this would be the last time I would ever bring it up. He gave me his same condolences as he hugged me back.

After I walked away from Ed, I thought about all that he had said to me, and I knew he was right. He had surely lost a lot more money than I had. Thank God, I had found my daughter that night, and fortunately, I had not lost four thousand dollars of my own money. After calculating the figures over and over in my mind as logically as I knew how to, I came up with the same amount as Ed had when it came to my losses that night. This thought also made me feel much better. Realistically, all I had really lost was **"two dollars and one ticket."**

Tootsie

Some things happen that we can't control;
We ask ourselves why, but we don't always know.

D.J. DeSai

My six-year-old daughter, Mindy, wanted her own puppy and pleaded with me for several months for one. I finally gave in to her while shopping at the mall one day. Mindy spotted a female wire fox terrier in a pet store and, honestly, I couldn't keep my eyes off the darling little puppy either. The pup was full of pep, radiating a lot of nervous energy, but I thought it was because she wanted a family just like us to take her home. Of course, I couldn't resist it, and bought her for a fair price of three hundred dollars. She came with papers proving that she was a full-blooded wire fox terrier. I also bought a cage for her, along with food and other necessities. Life was good for our little pet, and us, too. Mindy, my son Jake, and I had everything a family could want. We named the eight-week old, sweet puppy girl Tootsie.

Several months went by, proving that Tootsie was as nervous and full of energy as the day we had bought her at the mall. No amount of walking and running seemed to help. I was sure it was still the puppy in Tootsie, and I was also sure our pet would calm down as time went by. However, I cannot tell you how many times I took her out of her cage and tried to work with her, but it was useless. She was just too high-strung. She would not settle down no matter what, and I was getting so frustrated. She would jump up on everyone and everything, and I was left with not knowing what in the world to do with her. I wondered how much longer it would take Tootsie to relax so I could try to train her. All I could hope for was a better dog in time. Meanwhile, the children and I were miserable with our nervous pet.

Tootsie had bitten Mindy a few times, and the wounds were bad enough that she drew blood from her. I was afraid for my daughter to care for the pet; I feared that the dog would continue to bite her and maybe even become more violent and hurt her much worse. I knew Tootsie was only being a puppy and wanted to play, but she was way too rough. *The biting is much too extreme,* I thought.

I did not want, nor did I have the time, to care for the animal, and this was also not the deal that Mindy and I had previously made. Mindy was the one who had wanted the puppy and had promised me that she would take care of it. But I knew it was not Mindy's fault that Tootsie was so wild and could not be tamed. Although Mindy wasn't afraid of the puppy, I continued to worry about Tootsie biting her, so I took on most of the responsibility of taking care of the dog.

One day one of the neighbors yelled at me and said, "Dory, there is a dog training center located right down the road." At first I was offended, but after I thought about it for a minute, I was sure they were as aggravated with the pup as I was. I took my neighbor's advice constructively, hoping that Tootsie would benefit from some professional training.

Feeling somewhat excited, I started thinking there may still be some hope left after all for taming Tootsie. I called the training center to get some information, and after talking with the receptionist there I decided to enroll our pet for three weeks of training for the fair price of three hundred dollars. I figured I owed this much to all of us, especially Tootsie.

I really didn't care a lot for the puppy, but I didn't want to give her up either. I only wanted what any other pet owner would want, and that was a little peace of mind when it came to the puppy's behavior. *Maybe after Tootsie's training, she will make a wonderful pet,* I told myself. *Besides, I paid three hundred dollars the day I purchased her.* I would just look at the special training as an important investment for our pet. I was certain it would be money well spent.

Tootsie had to go away for three weeks of training. I must say that the homefront became quite peaceful again without her around. I hated to admit it, but I could have gotten very used to the quiet time really quickly. When the three weeks came to an end, I reluctantly drove to the training center to pick up our pet. I tried to get excited about picking Tootsie up, but I couldn't. I wasn't looking forward to taking her back home, because of all the consistent commotion she had caused. *Gee! Maybe she is a changed dog now,* I thought to myself.

When I arrived at the training center, I was surprised. Yes, I was very impressed with Tootsie's new tricks she had been taught. She knew how to sit and walk with a leash while using a little bit of grace. She was performing these few little actions with so much nervousness, though. This had me worried. The trainer said she would settle down some more after she got home. He said she had not gotten used to his place and for me to work with her for a few minutes every day. He showed me what to do. I told him I would do the exercises with Tootsie, and hoped it would work. I paid the trainer the three hundred dollars, and then drove home with our newly trained puppy.

For the next several days, I tried to work with Tootsie while rehearsing the drills the dog trainer had gone over with me. Sad to say, I was getting nowhere. Tootsie did not want to do anything for me. She started jumping, barking, crying, and running all over the place like before. I tried to hold her and to let her know I loved her but she did not want any part of it. It wasn't very long until the dog had gone back to the same exact behavior we had always known. She continued acting up with all the nervous energy she had before. She did not even act like a trained dog.

By this time, I was sorry I had purchased Tootsie, and sorry I had wasted the money for her training. I started thinking the only thing left to do was to put an ad in the newspaper and try to sell her. I didn't want to do this, but I was all out of ideas. I was growing so tired of letting everything else go while trying to deal with the hyper active animal. I decided the dog life was not for me, and I needed to come to terms with how I felt. I loved Tootsie, but I just couldn't tolerate her behavior any longer. I did not have the patience for this kind of dog, so I knew what I had to do. I had to put our dog up for sale. I would put an ad in the newspaper.

One week later, after the ad had come out, a nice woman called me and asked me if she could stop by and take a look at Tootsie. She said she was certain she wanted to purchase our dog because she had looked everywhere in the city for a breed just like her. I couldn't believe it! I told her yes, and then gave her directions to my home before we hung the phones up. *Wow! The lady is a godsend. She is an answer to my prayers. Yippee! Someone wants Tootsie, and someone will take very good care of her. It's my lucky day! It's Tootsie's lucky day, too!* I told myself.

In the ad, I had asked six hundred dollars for Tootsie because of the money I had invested in her. I was so pleased that someone was going to buy her and care for her. The lady said she was going to use Tootsie for breeding purposes. I did not care what her reason was. I only wanted the dog out of my life so I could have my peace of mind back again. I also wanted Tootsie to be happy too, although I knew she would never be happy living in my home. *How can the dog be happy if the owner isn't happy?* I wondered.

I began remembering back how Tootsie had gotten loose from her leash too many times. Quite often she would take off running like a fox. She would dart through the park across the street from my home and wreck people's dishes of food by jumping on their picnic tables. I had to endure the embarrassment of having to run after her and apologize to everyone for my dog ruining their family reunion or party. I would offer to pay for the damage, but most of the time everyone was very nice about it. I was just so tired of trying to settle down a dog that there seemed to be no hope for at all. I desperately needed a break. What I really needed was to sell Tootsie, and to be rid of her. Finally it was about to happen and I was so happy about it. I was sure Tootsie would be as happy in her new home as I would be without her in mine.

I heard a knock at the door, but I waited a minute so I wouldn't seem so overly excited. I opened the door with a big smile on my face so the dog-buyer would not know how unhappy I was. I also did not want the lady to know how unhappy she might be herself, after she bought Tootsie and took her home with her. I didn't really want to deceive anyone, but I only wanted someone to save me from a dog I could not control. *Maybe this lady can control Tootsie*, I hoped.

A couple of times, I had even thought about taking Tootsie to the dog pound, but I am not a cold-hearted person, so I did not have it in me to do this. Finally, I found myself free of all my negative thoughts. I was also very happy to be getting my money back I had spent on the dog. I could surely use it, and hopefully this woman would make some money, too, breeding Tootsie. I had hoped it would all work out for everyone, including the dog.

When I opened the door, I asked the lady to come in. She looked at Tootsie for a few minutes and then held her. She quickly said she wanted to buy her and asked me if I'd take a personal check as her payment. I didn't really want to take a check but I figured if I didn't, she may not have the cash to pay, and this might cause her to change her mind about buying Tootsie. I reluctantly told her the check would be fine.

Before the lady wrote the check, she asked me if she could bring Tootsie back to me in a couple of days if things did not work out as she had planned. I had never sold a dog before, so I made the mistake of telling the lady yes, while thinking again that she might change her mind about buying Tootsie if I told her no. The lady paid me, thanked me, and then left. I actually felt a little guilty about selling our dog, but I knew it was for the best, so needless to say, I was quick to forget the guilty thoughts after she was gone. Peace had come upon me, and it was sweet!

A few hours later, I heard a knock at my door. I opened it, thinking it was one of my friends or neighbors. *Oh no!* I thought to myself. *It's the lady who bought Tootsie, and she's struggling with all her might to hold on to the dog.* Tootsie was fighting so hard and squirming so much that it was becoming impossible for the lady to hold her down. The lady quickly threw Tootsie in my arms and then took a few steps backwards as if she couldn't wait to get away from the dog.

I felt a sick sense fall over my body when I heard the lady say that Tootsie was so beyond her control that she could not do anything with her. She said the dog would not settle down; she had never seen an animal this wound up before. She said that while counting all the dogs she had ever owned, Tootsie took the cake. She told me she thought the dog was so unhappy because she missed being with me. The lady said that Tootsie had most likely become very attached to me, and she had no choice but to bring her back. I knew every word she was speaking was not true, but I did not say anything. I just listened, but I was crying hard on the inside. *What in the world will I do with this dog now? How will I cope?* I wondered. The lady was feeling the same way I had been feeling for months.

Although I was so disappointed, I knew I had to keep my word like I told the lady I would. I gave her the check back and we quickly said our goodbyes. I wondered if anyone else would call me concerning the ad in the paper. If someone did call, I would know better the next time. I would tell them I wanted cash money and there would definitely be no refund under any circumstances whatsoever.

The following Sunday, my children and I went to church. This was about the only place I could find any peace of mind. I said a prayer that morning, and asked the Lord to answer me immediately concerning what to do about Tootsie.

When we returned home that afternoon, Mindy asked me if she could take the dog outside to play. I told her it was okay, but I firmly told her to be sure and securely tie her leash to something so she couldn't get loose and wreck someone else's picnic at the park. Mindy was quick to tell me she would not let Tootsie get loose.

I decided to take a hot bath while I was given a little alone time in the house. I knew Mindy would be bringing Tootsie back inside soon, so I'd better enjoy myself for a few short minutes. The dog was still yapping loudly twenty-four-seven, and would not sit still for any reason. She still required constant attention or she was not happy.

No one else had called concerning my ad in the paper, so I had just accepted the fact that we would include Tootsie in our daily lives and live with the consequences. I did not have the heart to take her to the pound, because I knew what might happen if I did. *No! I will keep the dog before I will allow anything bad to happen to Tootsie. Maybe she will calm down with time. Time can't come soon enough for me, though, so sad to say. There is nothing else to do about it, though,* I surely thought.

A few minutes had gone by while I was thoroughly enjoying my warm tub time. My feet had been aching most of the day from standing on them all week at work. Needless to say, this was just what I needed. Relaxation! It felt wonderful! I lay in the tub, closed my eyes, and thought about nothing for the next few minutes. I was in awe!

Suddenly, I heard Mindy running back into the house screaming as loudly as she could. I could hear her crying and shouting, "Mommy, Mommy! Something's wrong with Tootsie! She's hanging on the swing set and there's something dripping out of her mouth!" I jumped up from the tub as quickly as I could and looked out the bathroom window. "Oh my God," I whispered to Jesus. Tootsie was hanging in mid air from the swing set with nothing but the leash around her neck holding her up. Saliva was dripping down from her mouth and she wasn't breathing. I knew Tootsie had hung herself. She had strangled to death.

Mindy had tied Tootsie's leash to the swing set bar and walked away for only a short time. Tootsie had somehow managed to tangle her leash around the bars of the swing before she jumped back up on the swing's seat. Then she tried to jump to the ground from the swing again. Needless to say, there wasn't enough of the leash left for her to make it to the ground so she had hung herself in mid air. She was hanging there dead, and I felt so guilty. All the negative thoughts I had previously had about Tootsie did not seem too important now.

Although I knew our dog days with Tootsie were finally over now, I felt bad. Even though I would not have to care for the wild nervous animal anymore, I was saddened by her death. Even knowing that Tootsie was finally resting in peace, I still wished it wouldn't have ended this way. I wondered, though, if it were an answered prayer. Maybe it was God's will to put Tootsie out of her own misery and everyone else's. Maybe I was thinking some cruel thoughts, but I could not help it. If this was an act of God, I wondered if it was the best for all concerned, including Tootsie. God only knew.

A couple of the neighbors and a relative took Tootsie down from the swing set and carried her to the furthest part of the back yard. They covered her up with a blanket and we buried her a little while later. Mindy seemed the saddest of all, but I felt very blue, too. I knew my daughter was probably feeling guilty for leaving Tootsie close to the swing set and then walking off for a minute. I told her it was not her fault and that Tootsie had gone away to Doggie Heaven. Later, Mindy seemed better, so I felt certain she would be okay.

Since Tootsie's death, a few people have teasingly accused me of hanging the dog myself, but I didn't. Just because I had entertained the thought of it several times prior to the dog's death does not mean I would really do it. I wouldn't! I couldn't! Again, I didn't! My last prayer is, *rest in peace, finally,* **"Tootsie."**

Cold Hard Cash

If you think you've lost your secret stash,
Imagine finding cold hard cash.

D.J. DeSai

In this story, I compare my brain to a storage shed. Why? Because when I was younger, my mind had plenty of space to store things, just like an un-used storage shed has. During those earlier years I kept many things inside my head, and it did not take me long to remember something. From growing older, my storage shed has become very crowded and cluttered, so occasionally when I look for something or try to remember certain details, I've been known to have a memory lapse. Needless to say, this can very well cause a dilemma, as it did in this story.

One day I decided I'd better save some money or I would not be able to afford to take my two children on vacation that year. After saving for a few weeks, I counted one-hundred eighty dollars that I had left over from my last three or four paychecks. The thought crossed my mind that I'd better put it away somewhere safe to save for a trip or I might forget and spend it.

I had recently heard someone say that if you store money in your freezer, the chance of it burning would be very unlikely if your house ever caught on fire. I decided this was a good idea to try using on my vacation money. I knew I wouldn't need the cash for several weeks, and I wanted to store it somewhere safe.

When I arrived home from work one day, I carefully put the bills inside a zip-lock plastic bag. Then I zipped it up and headed for the freezer. I laid the bag underneath some frozen vegetables on the lower bottom tray. *This money will make for a very good start for a vacation savings,* I thought.

A few more weeks went by when I remembered I was supposed to be putting my extra money aside. Again, I took the left over saved up bills out of my purse, and then counted them. *Wow! I can't believe I have three-hundred twenty more dollars to add to my savings. We will be able to take a nice vacation if I keep this up,* I thought.

Feeling very happy, I stood there for a minute thinking about where I had put the money I had already saved. I checked a few places, but I couldn't find it. I stood in my living room for a while longer meditating. *What did I do with my money? I don't remember where I put it. I know I've already saved around two hundred dollars, but where is it? Did I spend it? If I spent it, what did I buy with it? Am I going crazy?* I asked myself. I thought about every little place I had previously hidden something, but there was no money anywhere to be found. I was getting tired of looking. *Oh well. It has to be somewhere,* I thought. *I'll find it later.*

The next few days I drove myself mad thinking about my lost vacation money. I was sure I had hidden it somewhere in my house. I started looking frantically in every wallet and purse I had. I un-zipped every zipper in every compartment and opened and searched every drawer in my home. I even looked in every pocket of every coat, shirt, and pants I had worn. I searched the entire house over and over. I also searched my car inside out, but still, the saved cash was nowhere in sight. After a while, I became mentally and physically exhausted thinking about the money and looking for it.

Finally, I decided to try to forget about it before I drove myself bonkers. There was nothing else I could do about it anyway, and there was no sense in torturing my mind anymore. I was so tired. I wondered if it was even worth what I was putting myself through. I would just have to try harder to save more money now that the time was drawing nearer for our trip. I didn't want to disappoint my children nor myself when it came to our vacation time. This was our escape from reality, and we all needed this so badly.

The next few weeks flew by, and then at last it was time for the three of us to pack. My two children were jumping up and down, excited about leaving, although we were not really going anywhere too extravagant. We were taking a trip to another state, but the state we were planning to travel to was located right next door to the one in which we currently lived.

I had reserved a hotel for a few days so we could swim during the day, go out to dinner at night, and maybe even catch a movie or two while we were away. I only wanted for all of us to hang out together and bond happily for a few days. Maybe I would take the kids shopping too, and we could go to a carnival one night. The children were never too picky about what we were doing as long as there was plenty of junk food to eat.

Sad to say, the trip came and went too soon. We had a great, relaxing time, though, which meant everything to me. I had stood on my feet every day at work, so getting away for a little rest and relaxation was the key remedy for me. Soon, it was back to work and school, though, but we all brought home some fond memories from our vacation.

The first week after we returned, I was watching the news one night when I heard an anchorman announce the name of a certain kind of refrigerator. Then I heard him say that the manufacturer was having a re-call because all the compressors were defective on that one particular model. I was sure my refrigerator was the one he was referring to. I had just bought it a few months prior to our trip.

The next day I called the company where I had purchased my refrigerator, and the sales clerk confirmed what the newsman had reported. He told me that there had been a re-call on mine after I read him the numbers off of my sales and warranty receipt. Once everything had been verified, the clerk said he would set up an appointment for me the following week. He apologized for the inconvenience and said, "Okay, Dory, will next Friday be suitable for you since the maintenance crew only works on week days?" I explained to him that I had to work that day too, but it should be fine. I told him that there would be someone at my home to let the crew in, but they would have to come between three and five o'clock in the afternoon. I knew my two children would be home after school with the babysitter then, so the time would work out okay. After the appointment had been set, we said our goodbyes.

On the day the maintenance crew arrived at my home, I got a call at my workplace from my son Jake. He was only nine years old, but he had shown a lot of responsibility that day. He had helped clean out the refrigerator before the men arrived to replace the compressor.

As I held the phone close to my ear, I could hear Jake laughing out loud while he told me about his job emptying the freezer. I wondered what in the world was so funny about that. In the past, Jake would fuss when he had to do an extra chore, so his behavior was very abnormal. I could hardly understand what my son was saying between his laughing and talking.

After Jake settled down from his excitement, he managed to remind me of the day I had lost some of my money. He remembered me frantically searching our home for the vacation money I had put away. As I stood there and thought about what Jake was saying for a moment, I suddenly remembered something very important. "Oh my God!" I blurted out, as I laughed back with my son thanking Jesus. I had finally recalled the money I had hidden from myself in the bottom tray of the freezer. Wow! It was all coming back to me now. Finally! I felt so silly, but so blessed.

With a big smile on my face, and feeling more than relieved that Jake had found the surprise stash in the secret place where I had hidden the lost treasure, I looked up to heaven and thanked my God again. I wondered how long it would have taken to find the money if my compressor had not gone out. I was sure it would have been a very long time and maybe never. Oh well! It did not matter now. Jake had found the money and this was all that mattered, because I was one-hundred eighty dollars richer than I had been the day before. I couldn't help but laugh out loud again, though, when Jake asked me if he could borrow two dollars of my **"cold hard cash."**

Belly Button and Ear Piercing Deal

No matter how you think you feel,
Be careful when you make a deal.

D.J. DeSai

There have been many times in my life when certain events and circumstances have proven to be huge lessons for me. However, there have been a few times when I have wished that some of them would have turned out differently. No matter, though: they are what they are. Therefore, I try to make the best out of them. Life's trials and tribulations, including the good, the bad, and the ugly, have probably happened for very good reasons. I think it is very important that we are growing every day in our lives from all that we go through.

My friend Henry and I decided to go to Florida one year during spring break. Henry had been given some unexpected time off at his workplace, and I just needed a little vacation. I was really looking forward to getting away from the weather, which had not been very pleasant in our city for several weeks. "A little sunshine is just what the two of us need," I told Henry laughingly. It was also a good time for me to take off from my business since so many of my clients would be vacationing with their families during spring break week, too.

Henry suggested to me that we rent a condo on the beach so we could spend our vacation time close to the ocean. I called a travel agency and luckily one of the agents found a two-bedroom condo that wasn't too costly, so by splitting the price equally between us, it seemed affordable enough. Excitedly, we could hardly wait for the day to arrive when we'd be leaving for the beach. We wanted to soak up the sun and have some fun.

With only one week left before the trip, I started packing my bags early, eagerly looking forward to getting away.

Finally, the time had arrived for us to leave. Henry picked me up early that morning, so we could make the ten-hour drive in one day. We were so happy and both of us were in a great mood. We laughed most of the way to Florida while listening to gospel, bluegrass, and rock music on the radio. I felt like a teenager again, footloose and fancy-free.

When we arrived at the condo that night, it was late. We took our suitcases up to our rooms, changed clothes, and walked down to the beach. What a cozy night it was. The water was cool, and the ocean was roaring with passion. Oh, how we loved it. Henry and I walked on the beach for awhile before deciding to go back up to our condo to call it a night. We were both very tired from the trip, so going to bed early while listening to the sound of the ocean was just what we needed.

We slept fairly late the next morning, waking up rested. We did not have to get up for anything or anyone. Once we finally did get up, though, we walked out the sliding door onto the balcony, and looked at the beautiful sunshine beaming down on the ocean's water. What a beautiful sight it was. Life seemed so perfect at that very moment.

A little while later, we went back into the kitchen and made ourselves some fresh coffee that the owners had left lying next to the coffee pot. We didn't have any food, so we decided we would go purchase a few items to eat for breakfast and lunch, since we would be there for the entire week. We agreed that we would eat dinner out in a restaurant every night, since we were both crazy about fresh seafood, and Florida was surely the place to be for this type food.

After we returned from the store, Henry and I put our groceries away. Then we put our bathing suits on, and took off to the beach with our cooler and beach bags. Life was wonderful. The two of us just sat there for a couple of hours reading our books we had brought with us. If we grew tired of reading, we would talk to each other or watch people. There were a lot of teenagers on the beach, and everyone seemed to be having a good time, or just lying around relaxing.

I was still feeling somewhat tired from the stress of my workplace. I really needed this vacation. Turning forty years old had hit me very hard, and I felt as though I couldn't do the things I used to do for lack of energy. I remember sitting on the beach, wishing so badly that I could be a teenager again, as I watched all the younger girls looking so young and appearing to be so vibrant in their bikini bathing suits. I couldn't help but feel envious of them. Maybe I should have felt better than I did about myself. My children and my friends had told me time and time again that, even though I was forty, I still looked great in a two piece bathing suit. I appreciated their compliments, although keeping my figure had required exercise. This was the main reason my stomach had remained fairly flat. Luckily, I did not have any stretch marks from having two babies. Most of my girlfriends had them, and they would tell me they were jealous of my belly. I found their comments very flattering, but I noticed their good qualities, too, and some of them I did not have.

Feeling the heat of the sun on our bodies, Henry and I decided we had been outside long enough, especially since it was our first day on the beach in Florida. We did not want to get sunburned, so we decided to go inside and have lunch. Later, we took a nap and then lounged around the rest of the afternoon talking and laughing before deciding we would go shopping at one of the malls before dinner.

We took our time getting ready. Then we drove to the mall, and walked around. We noticed a lot of shops in Florida that specialized in tattoos and body piercing. I couldn't believe how crowded all the businesses were. Gee, it seemed like everyone was getting something done to their body. Yes, this seemed to be the trend.

I looked at Henry and noticed he was watching everyone in awe too, just as I was. We found ourselves staring at a girl who had her nose, eyebrows, and tongue pierced. The teenage girl also had several holes in her ears, and one of her earrings looked as though it was as heavy as a bracelet. *Wow, I'll bet that earring hurts!* I thought to myself. We also saw a young boy who must have had one hundred tattoos all over his entire visible body. All he was wearing was a pair of shorts, but from what we could see, he was almost completely covered with ink. Henry said he could not believe the extremity of what some of the kids were doing to their bodies. He gazed at most of the teenagers in bewilderment. I couldn't help but think it was funny because my friend kept staring at all the people with his mouth wide open.

Henry was fifty years old, and he seemed to be a very old-fashioned man. I laughed out loud and I couldn't resist asking him teasingly why he didn't get one of his ears pierced. Henry told me that he was way too old to wear an earring. He laughed back at me while asking me why I didn't get a tattoo or a belly ring for myself. I told him I thought I was too old, too. We both laughed, as we decided to go inside the nearest bar to get a drink before dinner, since it was still fairly early and neither one of us was really hungry yet.

We ordered two beers and two shots of alcohol that the bartender convincingly suggested we try. The bartender said the shots were very popular drinks so Henry said, "Oh, what the heck!" He went on to tell the bartender that he and I were on vacation, so we needed to celebrate while making a toast to good times. Henry and I sat there drinking our drinks while we talked and laughed.

A few minutes later, Henry turned around and ordered two more beers and two more shots. "Wow! I'm not sure I should drink anymore," I told Henry. "I haven't drunk this much alcohol in quite some time." He started laughing and teasing me, telling me I needed to lighten up a little. I said, "Okay," as I drank the drinks down feeling a little light-headed. "Ooh," I mumbled. I was feeling so relaxed. I lay back in the chair, not feeling one single care in the world. *Maybe this is just what I need*, I thought.

After we finished our second drinks, Henry asked me if I wanted another round. Much to my surprise, I was quick to say yes. The drinks were making me forget about my job, my problems at home, and every other worry in the world I did not need, especially while I was on vacation. I knew my children and the rest of my family were okay, and they had actually been the ones to encourage me to take the trip. They said I needed some time away to forget everything for a few days. I sure was taking them up on their suggestions now, as I sat there feeling more than relaxed after the last drink. The alcohol had hit me hard and fast. I knew my limit and I was definitely there. "I certainly cannot handle another drink," I told Henry.

Both of us slowly got up from the chairs, paid for our drinks, and walked outside. I felt Henry put his arm around me. I asked him if I was staggering, feeling sure I was. Henry told me not to worry about it, as he laughed out loud. I looked up at him, and noticed his eyes were very blood shot. I told him we needed to walk for awhile, and get something to eat before we drove the car. "We need to sober up," I told Henry. He smiled, telling me we probably should have stopped after the first drink. I agreed. I couldn't help but smile back at him while asking him if he was ready for his tattoo or his ear piercing, as we continued to watch all the people again. Henry chuckled out loud and told me yes he was, if I was ready for my belly button ring. I laughed back, and teasingly told him I was ready. He said, "Okay, I'll do it if you'll do it." I said, "Okay, I'll do it if you'll do it." Suddenly, Henry grabbed my arm and led me into the closest shop. I laughed out loud. We were having the most carefree time we'd had in a very long time.

After we stepped inside the store, the owner walked over and asked if he could help us. We both laughed as Henry jokingly told the man which ear he wanted pierced. The owner did not waste any time sanitizing his ear. Then he grabbed the piercing gun and within a few short seconds, his ear was pierced. I looked at Henry and laughed, but he didn't laugh back. He looked stunned, as if he were in shock. I was worried about him, because, honestly, I was almost sure he was not really ready for the ear piercing. I was certain the man with the piercing gun had caught him off guard. The store owner was probably so used to doing his job that he didn't waste any time doing it. I couldn't help but believe that Henry's piercing suggestion had just been the alcohol talking. It was not really like him. I would have bet money that he wasn't one-hundred percent serious about the piercing but it was too late to think about it now. It was a done deal.

Wow! Henry was still standing there looking as though he had seen a ghost. I heard his voice tremble when he said, "Okay Dory, it's your turn now." We both started laughing again as I said, "Oh, I don't think so. I'd better not do that." I told Henry I was just thankful he was alright from the ear piercing, and that I would be alright, too, without the belly ring. Henry was quick to say, "No way, Dory!" He told me that we had made a deal, and we were not going to leave the store until I got my belly button pierced. We laughed again, but this time my laugh wasn't as persuasive as before. I thought about Henry's comment for a quick moment and then told him okay. I felt bad that he had gone through with the ear piercing, so I knew it would make him feel better if I got the piercing, too. It didn't seem like a big deal anyway. I decided to do it for him.

We followed the owner to the back of the store. The man told me he had already pierced at least ten other girls' belly buttons that same day, so this made me feel a little more relaxed. *At least he's experienced,* I thought. I told the owner I had decided to go ahead and go for it, since I had jokingly told my friend I would. Honestly, though, I couldn't help but think the belly button ring was kind of cool. I remembered seeing it on so many of the teenage girls who were walking on the beach. *Besides, how badly can a little hole in my belly button hurt?* I asked myself. *I've already had both my ears pierced several years prior, so this can't be any worse than that. It might even make a forty year old woman feel a little younger,* I told myself. At least, I had hoped it would. Yes, I had talked myself right into it and I felt I deserved it. *I will do this for myself and I will end up loving it,* I decided.

As I stood there, I pulled my long tee shirt all the way up and told the owner of the store to go ahead and pierce my belly button. He laughed, telling me I would have to lie down. I wondered why I'd have to lie down, as he led me to a private room. *Surely he'll just get his piercing gun out and shoot me with it really fast and easy,* I told myself. *Won't it be as simple as what mine and Henry's ear piercing had been?* I wondered. I was starting to feel a little uncomfortable by then, especially since the alcohol was slowly wearing off. It didn't seem as funny to me as what it had been before.

The store owner laid me all the way back in a chair. I found myself lying on something similar to a dental chair. Then I saw the man get a very large needle out, looking as though he were getting ready to perform a serious surgery. The very second I decided I would jump up from the chair and not follow through with our piercing agreement, the store owner began sticking the long needle deep into my skin. "Oh my God!" I cried out to the Lord. "That hurts!" It felt nothing like my ear piercing had felt. All I could manage to do was lie back down and deal with the pain of the needle that was traveling from the outer layer of my skin to the inside layer. The needle was penetrating from the bottom of my belly button all the way back through to the top. "Ouch!" I moaned. "This is really hurting badly!" All I could think about was when he would finally be finished sticking that gigantic sword of a needle inside my belly. It felt like he was never going to get the piercing completed, but I managed to notice that he was also pulling a large strand of thread through. The thread was attached to the needle. I was guessing he needed to make sure the hole was large enough for the ring to go all the way in. No matter, I could hardly stand it. It hurt so badly! I said a silent prayer.

After the store owner had finished the piercing and the belly button hole had definitely been made, he still had to put the ring in and pull it back through to fasten it. This procedure was no picnic either. All the while, I could not believe I had done something so silly and so hurtful to myself. I was still partly numb from the alcohol, although now I felt numb from the shock of the needle. Thank God! The pain started easing up.

I looked up at Henry to find him looking as white as a ghost. He told me he was so sorry, because he had no idea it would hurt me like that. He kept telling me not to worry, because he was there with me. He promised me that he would not leave me. I thanked him, and I was so glad when it was over. I managed to raise myself up, while Henry helped me out of the chair. My belly was so sore that I couldn't even fasten my blue jean shorts back. Henry paid the man for both services, and then we quickly left the store. Needless to say, neither one of us was laughing anymore. The alcohol had worn off now, so we could both feel the pain.

We walked to the car and slowly got in. I knew we were completely sober so there was no danger whatsoever in either one of us driving the car. Henry kept apologizing to me over and over again for the pain I had endured. He told me he had almost passed out from watching the entire ordeal. I told him it was not his fault, and that I would be okay, even though I was wishing I had not done it. Henry told me that his ear was not hurting much anymore, and he was glad he had gotten it pierced. "It makes me feel a little younger," he told me.

We stopped to get something to eat before we headed back to the condo. Afterwards, we felt somewhat better, although I still could not fasten my pants all the way. My piercing was so sore! I was very thankful that I had worn a long tee shirt that night. It hung down far enough to cover my unfastened pants and my red swollen belly button.

I was wishing I would have at least waited until our last day vacationing to do what I did, because my belly button stayed red and inflamed for the rest of the week. I wondered if it would get infected, and sure enough it did. When we got back home, it was a mess. I noticed some pus coming out of it, so I went to the drugstore to ask the pharmacist what he suggested I use to clear it up. He told me what to buy. He also told me to treat the infected area several times a day.

For the next few weeks, I applied the ointment to my piercing. I nurtured my belly button and finally, it started to heal. I was also able to fasten my jeans again, thank God. It had been several weeks since I had been able to do this, and afterwards, it actually felt odd to fasten them. I wondered if the piercing was worth what I had been through.

Would I do this again? No. Do I love my belly button ring? Yes. Have I had any problems with it since the infection? Yes and no.

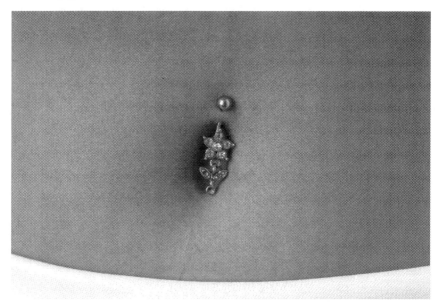

I have had three major surgeries since then and before each one, I had to go to a piercing specialist to have the ring removed. It was doctor's orders. Finally, though, I got smart and purchased a belly ring I could put on and take off myself. Now, it is not a big deal to remove it. Once it healed, I haven't had another problem with it, thank God.

Henry and I can finally laugh about our wild event in Florida. Our wounds are completely history now, enabling us to enjoy our dual piercing. One thing is for sure, though: we made a very fond memory for ourselves while we were on our spring break vacation. Now, when either one of us is asked which one got the short end of the stick or the fat end of the needle, as I call it, we both agree I did. Yes, I was the victim when it came to the **"Belly button and ear piercing deal."**

Lucky, Unlucky Numbers

It can cost you a fortune to make a mistake,
So try and correct it before it's too late.

D.J. DeSai

Do you ever wonder why certain things happen the way they do? When we are faced with decisions and use the best of our knowledge to make them, sometimes they turn out for the best, but oftentimes we choose the wrong roads and make mistakes along the way. All of these right and wrong turns can really change the entire picture of just about any situation in life. I guess this is what makes the world keep turning, and as long as we are learning and growing every day, this should be all that matters.

One day during my lunch hour at work, I walked over to a nearby neighborhood store. I felt the need to get away from my business for a few minutes, but I also wanted to browse the store. This certain shop carries a little bit of everything, and I am always so amused each time I go in. I get caught up in all the merchandise they sell and what it is used for. I'm like a kid in a candy store trying to look at everything I possibly can in just a few short minutes.

On this one particular day, I noticed some items sitting on a big table, so I started skimming through them to see if I could find a good deal on one I may be interested in. *Everything on the table is on sale for fifty percent off, so how can I resist this? After all, a sale is surely my best friend,* I thought to myself.

Grabbing a horoscope book, I noticed my Virgo sign on the front of it. It looked straight at me as if to say, "Pick me up and read me," so I did. I skimmed through it for just a brief moment, looking at it long enough to notice a lucky number chart printed toward the back of the book. I read the Virgo's numbers out loud. My lucky numbers were listed as four, three, eight, and one. Hurriedly, I put the book down while looking at the clock on the wall. I was running out of time so I decided I would memorize the four lucky numbers written in the book. I made a mental note in my mind that I would try my luck with the Virgo numbers the next time something came up that had to do with gambling.

I had never really believed in horoscopes, but I decided I might try it just once. I didn't really think it was right to gamble either unless I was only doing it for fun every once in awhile. Out of boredom or for some reason or another, I was ready to try something different for a change.

Later that afternoon, I left work with more energy than when I went in. When I got home, I thought I'd just relax, but when I sat down on my sofa, I couldn't sit still. I was too restless. I got up, deciding to call my friend Luke. When he answered the phone, I asked him if he'd like to ride over to a place called The Downs with me. The Downs is a horse race track located in our town, and the two of us had been there together a couple of times already, and we loved it.

Luke answered the phone sounding thrilled that I had called. He immediately said, "Yes, Dory, I'd love to go with you." During this kind of harness race, the horses pull buggies while the horse jockeys ride in the buggies, controlling the horses while they run in the race. It almost seems impossible to pick the winner of one of these races, because there are times when the horses break stride in the beginning of the race. Sometimes they just don't feel like running.

The last time Luke and I went to the track, we each threw dice to determine what numbers we would bet on instead of trying to figure out the winner by reading the program or the racing form. The way we decided the horse numbers we would bet on depended on the number the dice landed on. Then we would bet and box those two numbers. A box bet meant that both our horses had to win and come in second place. It didn't matter which horse came in first or which one came in second, as long as both of them came in. We had agreed that we had just about the same chance of winning by doing it this way as any other way. Believe it or not, we had rolled the dice and went home winning money before.

I drove to Luke's house to pick him up, and from there I drove to the track. As soon as we made our way in, Luke pulled the dice out of his pocket. We each rolled one, one at a time. The number I rolled and the number Luke rolled would tell us which two numbers we would bet during each race. We would box the two numbers, and this bet was called an exacta box. If the two horses came in first and second either way, then we would win and split the winnings between the two of us.

The night was almost over and we had not won anything yet. We had only bet two dollars each on each race so we had not lost much either, but we were sure having a good time drinking a couple of beers, talking, and just hanging out together. Luke and I were very good friends.

We were coming up on the last race of the night when I heard the track announcer say that if anyone wanted to place his wages on a bet called the superfecta, there was still thirty minutes left to do it. He also said there was carry-over money in the pool for this particular bet, totaling fifty thousand dollars. Evidently no one had purchased a winning ticket for the past few nights so the money had accumulated. In order to win it, someone has to pick four horses in the same race and all four of these horses has to come in first, second, third, and fourth. The track announcer also went on to say that because the money pool was so high, they were going to guarantee giving the fifty thousand dollars away, even if no one picked all four horses to come in. He said they would pay the superfecta money out on three wins with all, which meant I could box four horses, but only three of them had to come in first, second, and third. It did not matter about the fourth horse as long as I had the first three in the correct sequence. Of course, if anyone picked all four horses to come in the money, the three horse win would not be valid.

Gee! I thought to myself. *Even though the ticket office is guaranteeing three wins with all, it will still be a tough combination to pick. Fifty thousand dollars is certainly a lot of money, though,* I decided. *I wish I could win it since Luke and I have not even cashed a ticket all night. How in the world can I possibly pick three horses to come in the money when we can't even pick two?* I wondered. Nevertheless, I couldn't help but wonder if I should spend a couple of extra dollars and bet the big superfecta. I had too many thoughts going through my mind.

It was my turn to go get our ticket for the last race, so I decided I would go ahead and purchase a superfecta ticket for myself since the pool money was up so high. I made up my mind that I would spend only two dollars and get a straight bet just to keep it simple and inexpensive.

All of a sudden a delightful and exciting thought came to my mind as I remembered the lucky numbers that I had seen earlier in the horoscope book at the store while I was shopping on my lunch hour. I couldn't wait to use those same numbers for my superfecta bet. After all, the chart inside the book told me the numbers four, three, eight, and one were my lucky Virgo numbers, and I still had them memorized vividly in my mind. I was sure this must be the right time to bet on them. *Maybe this is a sign, and I will win the big fifty thousand dollars,* I thought to myself. This idea brought a big smile to my face.

Wow! I was so excited when it was finally my turn to bet. I purchased mine and Luke's exacta box ticket first, and then I told the teller I wanted a two-dollar straight superfecta bet, as I silently tried to remember my lucky Virgo numbers. I was feeling so eager and the crowd was so noisy that I had to think for a second before I spoke. Feeling a little rushed and confused I went on to say, "I want the numbers three, four, eight, and one." The teller printed the ticket out for me, and I paid him before leaving the cashier window.

Oh no! I thought to myself, after walking away and looking at my ticket. The numbers that I had told him I wanted were correct on the ticket, and they were also the same numbers in the horoscope book, but I had not recited them the same way they were written in the book. The numbers were not in the right order. I should have said I wanted four, three, eight, and one; instead I told him I wanted three, four, eight, and one. I had put the number three before the four, and this was not the way the numbers were written in the book.

I wanted to exchange my ticket and have the cashier reprint it the correct way, but by this time a man behind me had already started his betting transaction. The line was also very long. I decided the ticket I was given, right or wrong, would have to do this time. I was not going to stand back in that long line again, and I was probably just being silly for thinking that the numbers would really bring me that much luck anyway. Again, I didn't really believe in horoscopes, so why was I making such a big deal over the silly numbers? I talked myself right out of changing my ticket or purchasing another one with the numbers I had seen written in the back of the book. Feeling fidgety, I started walking back to where Luke and I were sitting.

I stopped to pick up more drinks for the two of us, but this time I ordered two non-alcoholic beverages. I also picked up a couple of sandwiches, because we had drunk a couple of beers on empty stomachs. We needed something else in our bellies before going home. I knew Luke would thank me later.

The last race was getting ready to run. As I handed Luke his drink and sandwich, I told him that I had gotten a superfecta bet for the last race.

I also told him about the lucky numbers I had read about in a book that same morning. Luke laughed and said, "You never know, Dory! You could be the winner." He told me that it was very hard to pick that many horses to come in the money. He asked me if I had boxed them, and I told him no. I told him I didn't even recite the numbers to the teller the way I had meant to. Luke laughed again as I explained to him what had happened when I got up to the window. He told me not to feel bad, because he doubted it mattered much anyway. He told me that my chances of winning were slim to none. I agreed, and we got ready to watch the race.

The horses took off with their buggies and jockeys behind them as I sat there feeling anticipation, and waiting, hoping, and wondering if Luke and I were going to have the winner of the last race. When the race was over, we both decided we had come close to winning because one of our horses had come in the money, but not the other one. "Close only counts in horse shoes and not horse races," I shouted out to Luke. We both teased each other, as we laughed. One of our horses had come in second or third we thought, but the other one was too far back, so we knew we had not won the exacta race. All we could see at the finish line was most of the horses bunched close together. They were all trying to be the one to make it there first and then on to the winner's circle. Luke and I only knew that the winners were not the same numbers we had rolled with the dice. "Oh well! Better luck next time, Dory!" Luke shouted to me. We had only lost a few bucks while having a great time, so it didn't matter a whole lot anyway.

The two of us sat there and talked for a few minutes while waiting for the traffic jam to clear from the parking lot. Soon we heard the announcer say that the race was now official, so we both looked up at the board to view the winning numbers that were posted. The number four horse had won; the number three horse had come in second; and the number eight horse had finished third. Luke and I had rolled the number two and the number eight with the dice, so we knew we had not won anything. It was time to go home.

All of a sudden my heart skipped a beat when I realized that my three lucky horoscope numbers were posted on the board. All I could do was gaze in bewilderment. I was looking at the number four, the three, and the eight. I didn't know which horse had come in fourth, but it didn't really matter because the announcer had said they were paying out the big money on three wins with all. This meant any number could come in fourth, as long as no one else had picked the first four horses to come in the money.

I felt a sick feeling fall in the pit of my belly, along with excitement and fear all at the same time. Just as I was about to tell Luke about the numbers on the board, I looked up and saw what the pay-off was. The race was official, and the carry-over pay-off was twenty-eight thousand dollars. "Oh my God," I whispered to Jesus. *Could this be a blessing from above?* I wondered. All four of my numbers were clearly posted. The Lord knew I'd been struggling lately paying the bills, so maybe this was a gift from him. After all, I was not a compulsive gambler, so I didn't believe that betting for fun was wrong.

Wow! I wondered if my ticket were any good, because on my ticket I had the numbers three and four in the wrong places. "Oh no," I whispered to myself. After thinking about it, I was almost sure I had not won. I wanted to kick myself for not getting back in line to get my ticket reprinted the way the numbers had read in the horoscope book. At least I could have taken the time to buy another two-dollar ticket with the same numbers in the right sequence. I just felt like crying, but what could I do now? All I could think was, *I can't believe all my lucky Virgo numbers, which are four, three, eight, and one, are posted on the board, and in that same exact order. I have a feeling these four numbers will haunt me forever.*

Sitting there with my heart in my lap, I told Luke what had happened, and he could not believe it either. We looked at my ticket and the numbers were printed plainly. The ticket read three, four, eight, and one. I had all of the right numbers that were posted on the board, but they were not in the correct order. Luke told me I should have boxed the four numbers. I told him it would have cost way too much, and I did not have or want to gamble that much money. He said he understood, but he knew I must be feeling so bad. He told me he was sure I didn't win anything, but if it would make me feel better, we'd walk up to the window to check the ticket anyway. He said it might ease my mind. He also said we should make absolutely sure the ticket was or wasn't a winner before we left to go home.

As soon as the two of us showed my ticket to the teller who was working the window, the first words that came out of his mouth were, "Oh my goodness! Why didn't you box these four horses?" He said that I could have boxed all four numbers for a one-dollar bet, and it would have cost only a total of twenty-four dollars. He said if I'd spent the extra money to box the four horses for a one-dollar bet, I'd still have won half of what the pay-off was.

"Man! Oh man!" Luke and I whispered. I walked away from the cashier window feeling worse than I already had. I was wishing I'd left it alone. I was so down. *What is the difference in winning twenty-eight thousand dollars or half of that?* I thought to myself. Happily, I would have taken either one. The money was mega no matter how I looked at it. Honestly, though, I was almost certain that I would not have bet twenty-four dollars on one horse race. The main reason I was so aggravated with myself was because I had not followed my heart concerning the betting of my lucky numbers. After all, I had recognized my mistake concerning the ticket, but I decided not to correct it. I may have won twenty-eight thousand dollars by only betting two more dollars.

Needless to say, all the number figures kept flashing through my mind, although I had not won anything. *Oh well! What does it matter?* I asked myself. *There is nothing anyone can do about it now. There is no sense in beating myself up anymore over it. It is finished,* I finally decided.

Luke and I headed for home. When I dropped him off at his house, he told me he was so sorry about my losing ticket and I knew he meant it. I thanked him and told him I was okay and that we would talk later.

On my way home, there were a few questions that kept running through my mind. *Would I have won the money if I had said the numbers the way I meant to say them? Or would that have changed everything, including the entire horse race? Who knows?* I thought. *The only thing I really know for certain is that I did not win, so obviously I wasn't meant to. Were the numbers really supposed to be lucky for me?* I wondered. Since I didn't win the money betting on the so-called lucky numbers, probably because I didn't rehearse them the way they were written in the book at the store, I simply can't resist calling them my **"Lucky, unlucky numbers."**

What a Trip

Learning from others may not be the best,
So search for your answers before the test.

D.J. DeSai

Finding yourself in an embarrassing situation can sometimes turn out to be funny many years later. Thank God, life is full of so many lessons too, especially when we get ourselves in those little pickles we sometimes hate. I wouldn't want to find myself in that same place over and over again, though. Sometimes, once is more than plenty.

Also, listening to other people can cause trouble if we don't scope out the truth of the matter first. Everyone has an opinion, and someone else's is not always the one to follow. In this story, I had to learn that the hard way, though I did learn, thank God.

While planning my very first trip out of the country, I was overly excited. I had heard so much about Cancun, Mexico, and finally, I was preparing for a trip to go with my best friend, Clark. It was an all inclusive, seven day, seven night trip, and we had gotten a great deal on a special package price.

Before deciding to go, I talked to several people, including a few of my clients and my travel agent who had all been to this land of paradise before. Everyone was sure to tell me how beautiful it was. There was also something else that they all kept telling me time and time again. "Dory, this is very important information that you had better not forget," they all said. "Under no condition whatsoever should you drink the water there." They said it would be easy for anyone from our country to get sick from drinking the water in Mexico, because our bodies are not accustomed to it. They also told me that I shouldn't eat the fruit or the raw vegetables, because the food is washed with their own water. "By drinking the water or eating the uncooked foods, you will most likely get sick," they said.

This part of the trip sounded somewhat depressing to me, because if I were to become sick, it would definitely ruin my vacation. These same people also made a point of telling me to be very careful not to do anything wrong while I was there, or I may get locked up in a Mexican jail. "Dory, this is somewhere you do not want to go," they told me. "Mexico's culture and laws are so much different from ours," they said.

All of this advice seemed simple enough at the time, because I was really looking forward to going. I couldn't wait! I knew I was not going to do anything wrong there to jeopardize my vacation. I just wanted to get away, have a good time, and relax on the beach.

I must have packed fifteen outfits in my suitcase along with ten pairs of shoes, and one hundred other accessories. *I have to be sure and pack everything I might need and want for my trip, because Cancun is my dream vacation,* I thought. *I do not want anything to go wrong.* While I was packing, I also thought about the water and fruit that I could not have while I was there. I wondered if I could make it for an entire week without these two items, because I would be out in the hot sun a lot of the time. I was certain the water and fruit would help keep me from getting so dehydrated. *I also love fruit, and it's very healthy,* I told myself. *I'm sure the resort will have bottled water, but I wonder if I should take a few extra ones with me. It can't hurt,* I decided. The more I thought about everything I had been told, the more my desire for fruit and water increased. "Wow! I'm so thirsty just thinking about not having any," I whispered to myself.

The day before the trip, I went to the store and bought a bag of oranges, a bag of assorted apples, and a bunch of bananas. While I was there, I went ahead and bought some bottled water to take with me, too. When I got home I threw the water and most of the fruit in an extra suitcase, because all I could think was, *better safe than sorry.* I felt sure if I were deprived of one of these items when I got there, I would be glad that I had brought some of them with me. *Besides, Clark and I can eat the fruit and drink the water while we're there for a week, and when the time comes to pack and go home, I can use the extra suitcase for my souvenirs,* I thought. *Yes, everything is going to work out just fine,* I smiled to myself. *I'm so happy that I know so many people who are nice enough to let me in on some of the little things I don't know.* Yes, I felt very grateful, and I believed I finally had all the bases covered. Everything seemed to be coming together concerning the trip. I was on cloud nine awaiting our vacation. I knew it would be filled with nothing but paradise, relaxation, and fun.

Clark and I had to be at the airport two hours before our flight left the next morning. We didn't get much sleep that night so five o'clock came quickly. Our plane was scheduled to leave at eight that morning. We were so tired by the time we lugged everything around at the airport, took care of our paperwork, and checked our suitcases. Then we had to go through another check line with our carry-on bags, which were filled to the max, too. I was wishing I had packed a little lighter, because the carrying of the luggage had worn me out, and it was still so early yet. Oh well. I felt as though I needed everything I had brought, so I knew I'd be glad when we got there and I had it with me.

Feeling somewhat overwhelmed, I was still wondering if I'd forgotten anything while thinking about getting on the plane. I had always been a little claustrophobic in the past, so while Clark and I were waiting for our flight, I decided to buy myself a mixed drink to calm my nerves. I drank it quite quickly, because I knew there wasn't much time to spare before we had to board.

Finding our seats on the plane didn't take long. Clark and I were among the first in line, so we were seated promptly. Then we had to wait on everyone else to get on. After sitting there for a few minutes, I wondered why everything seemed to be getting so tiny. It seemed as though the plane was closing in on me. There wasn't much room. I couldn't help but think of a movie I had just watched a few nights prior. The movie was about passengers who had to get off the airplane immediately, because it was about to blow up. These negative thoughts made me wonder how in the world I would exit the plane quickly enough if there were an emergency situation, as the one in the movie.

All of a sudden I started panicking. All I could think of was how I could get off the plane before it took off. "Oh my God! Help me Lord!" I prayed. I had scared myself to death, and the alcohol I had drunk was not helping matters any. It was making me feel more paranoid than calm. My heart was pounding so fast, and I couldn't breathe very well. I was having an anxiety attack.

Feeling petrified, I knew there was no time to waste. I looked at Clark and told him I had to get off the plane right now. Clark asked me what was wrong. I told him I did not know. He tried to calm me down, but no matter what he said, it did not work. I grabbed my purse and started to get up from my seat when I looked down at a little boy sitting right next to me. He looked to be around seven years old. Thank God he spoke to me or I would not have flown that morning. The little boy asked me if I was okay. I was sure he saw the fear written all over my face. I did not want to scare him, so I casually told him I had changed my mind about going on the trip. He asked me if I was afraid. I said, "Yes, just a little." I couldn't help but smile when the little boy said, "Don't be scared, lady. This kind of plane has never crashed." The child must have shocked the fear right out of me because I started calming down by the words he had spoken to me. I couldn't believe the sweet little youngster was acting so brave compared to a grown woman like myself. *I'm really ashamed of my behavior,* I thought. I took a deep breath, thanked him, and told him I was okay, as I closed my eyes and tried to think of something more pleasant. I wondered if his parents had heard our conversation. I was so embarrassed, feeling like a child myself.

My anxiety attack was finally subsiding. This had happened to me a few times in the past so I knew what I was dealing with, and I also knew I would be okay in time. I told myself I was going on this trip come heck or high water so I sat there and made myself relax. I started taking deep breaths, slowly breathing in and out, as the plane started climbing higher and higher in the air.

We flew to Florida first, and the flight went well. Clark and I grinned at each other when the plane landed safely. All of the passengers, including the two of us, got off the plane for about an hour before picking up some more passengers. Then we all re-boarded and took off for Cancun. I hated getting back on the plane again, but I started getting excited just knowing we were getting closer to the beautiful blue water and beach. Oh, I couldn't wait!

About an hour before the plane was to land in Cancun, the flight attendants came around with a customs form for each passenger to fill out. The form asked if passengers were carrying any kind of live plant, vegetable, fruit, or animal. "Oh my God!" I prayed again. *Why are the authorities asking these questions? Am I going to get into trouble for bringing my fruit?* I wondered. I just sat there for a few minutes and wondered why they would care if I had brought my own fruit from home if I couldn't eat any of their fruit while vacationing.

I decided to ask another lady passenger what the form was all about. The lady told me that no one was allowed to bring any of the items listed on the form out of the country into another country. *Oh my goodness!* I thought. *What in the world am I going to do now?* All I could imagine at this point was the Mexican jail I had heard so much about. *Gee! Will I even make it to Cancun before they lock me up?* I wondered. I just sat there with my heart beating a mile a minute while wondering what I was supposed to do. I asked Clark what he thought about it, but he didn't know either. I was sure he was scared for me, too, and was probably wishing he had taken the trip with someone else.

One of the flight attendants walked by, so I frantically stopped her, and told her about the fruit problem. She chuckled out loud. I asked her what was so funny. She said she couldn't believe all those people had told me I couldn't eat the fruit in Cancun. She said it was fine to eat their fruit. She also said there would be plenty of bottled water there to drink, so I should not have brought any of those items with me. I asked her what I was supposed to do now. She told me to just fill out the form and write down that I did not have any of those things with me. She assured me that everything would be okay. I went ahead and did what the flight attendant told me to do, although I felt very guilty, because I knew I was telling a lie. My fruit and water had been checked in and stored inside one of my suitcases, and this was the truth.

I worried for the next several minutes. When the plane landed in Cancun, I felt as though I were glued to my seat. Clark didn't move either. We just sat there and let all the other passengers go ahead of us until we were the last two people left seated on the plane. Clark was looking very aggravated by then, and this made me feel even worse. I decided to say another prayer, asking the Lord for help.

It didn't take long for the flight attendant to walk back to ask me and Clark what our problem was. When I reminded her of the forbidden fruit again, she told me to give it to her so she could throw it away. I told her it was packed in one of my suitcases that I had checked in at the airport, and I did not have access to it. She said, "Oh no! I thought you had the items with you in your carry bag." "No," I said. "This is why I'm so worried." The flight attendant said, "Come on, lady! You don't know how bad I want a cigarette. If you did, you would get up and get off of this plane now." She seemed aggravated with me too, instead of concerned. *Great!* I thought. *I'm on my own now, and I'm scared to death. I'll probably get locked up in the Mexican jail house and never get to go back home again.* I was so frightened!

Forcing myself to get up from my seat was not easy, and what I saw when I got off the plane was not a pretty picture. I could see security guards and Mexican policemen standing there holding their guns, looking as if they were ready to shoot someone if they needed to. Clark was trying to console me, but for some reason I was not feeling much better. I was truly afraid of what might happen next.

The two of us had a short distance to walk before picking up our luggage and leaving the airport. I was still worried to death, especially while I was being approached by several Mexicans who were speaking Spanish. I could not understand what in the world they were saying to me. I was sure they were all trying to tell me that they knew I had the fruit inside my suitcase, and that I was going to go to jail because of it. I kept trying to communicate with them as politely as I knew how to, but I still could not comprehend what they were trying to say. I did not understand or speak Spanish. I just kept walking as fast as I could, hoping and praying they were not telling me I was going to jail.

All the way through the airport, as Clark and I were trying to get out as fast as we could, we knew something was wrong. The Mexican people would not leave us alone. I was still sure they were trying to confront me about the fruit, but Clark kept hurrying me to the exit doors. So afraid, I kept walking fast, waiting in agony to be handcuffed, and taken in at any given moment. I was also sure they had professional dogs that could sniff out my fruit just as I had heard they could smell drugs. *What have I gotten myself into?* I wondered. *I'm so afraid!*

Thank God, Clark and I finally made it to the bus which was to take us to our resort. After I sat down, I heard the tour guide apologizing to everyone concerning the time share sellers who had been harassing everyone inside the airport. *Oh great!* I thought, as I looked at Clark sitting there with a big grin on his face. Then he started chuckling out loud. I tried to laugh with him, but I couldn't yet. I was more grateful, though, than anyone will ever know. "Thank the Lord I am not getting locked up for fruit reasons," I told Clark. "The Mexicans inside the airport were only trying to sell us time shares." It was quite funny after I thought about it, but I still didn't feel like laughing. I was too stressed out.

Gee! I really needed to calm down. I was so appreciative when someone asked me if I wanted a Corona beer. Yes! That was just what I needed, even though my last alcoholic drink that morning at the airport had just about done me in. Still, I was more than ready to try it again. Clark joined me in having a Corona beer, and we toasted to our vacation.

As the bus driver drove off from the airport, and headed for our hotel, I saw more Mexican men standing guard with their guns. By this time, though, the Corona had kicked in and I wasn't worried anymore. I was ready to have a good time, and no one was going to rain on my parade for one whole week. "Yippee!" I screamed.

Clark and I hung out at the beach and pool for the next few days. I was still afraid to eat the native fruit so I ate my own, still feeling as though I were committing a crime by having it with me. Finally after a few days, I decided it didn't matter. I saw everyone else eating the fresh fruit so I tried the pineapple, and it was delicious. I didn't get sick, so I was wishing I had not listened to anyone else. I had only cheated myself. Life is full of lessons, and this was just one of them for me. I would know better the next time.

I loved shopping at all the different places while we were there and, of course, I bought too many things to take back home. It didn't matter, though, because I had the suitcase I had brought the fruit in. I had plenty of extra room to store the souvenirs. The fruit would be eaten and the suitcase would still be used. Life was wonderful in Cancun.

The entire stay had been awesome, but soon it was time to pack and think about leaving. Our vacation had gone by so quickly, but I was starting to get a little excited about getting home and seeing my family and my dogs. I missed them all so much.

Needless to say, I did not wear half of the clothing or the shoes that I had taken with me. I still felt more secure, though, just knowing I had them. Again, I would do things a little differently the next time. This was my first trip out of the country, but I would be a pro from now on. Lo and behold, it took me forever to pack my suitcases to go home, and now it was time for me to lug all of my life around for another whole day. I was surely not looking forward to carrying the luggage again, and going through customs at the airport.

That morning after Clark and I had gotten on the plane, we were exhausted again. As the plane was taking off, Clark was laughing about how I had practically packed my entire closet. It felt so good to laugh versus having an anxiety attack. I knew that Clark was trying to make me forget my previous claustrophobic behavior, because he was afraid of a reoccurring attack. I was very grateful for this so I thanked him.

Clark reminded me that we were to land in Florida, get off the plane, check our bags, and then go through customs. I was not looking forward to any of this, because I had overheard people talking about this certain procedure being a big hassle. I also remembered how stressed out I had become the day that we had flown to Cancun. I figured, though, that since I had made it through the fruit deal, I could make it through anything now.

I filled out the customs form, but this time, I felt much more secure. I wrote down every item I had purchased in Cancun, which included many souvenirs for my family and friends. I had also bought some Mexican blankets, a large ceramic bird, and a beautifully hand-painted flower vase for myself. I had carefully wrapped some of my breakable items using my own clothing in my suitcase, so nothing would get broken.

Soon we got off the plane, picked up our luggage, and headed for customs. We had to take all our bags through a long line to have them randomly checked. As I was entering the room where the security guards were standing, I looked up and noticed a very tall man dressed in a suit walking toward me. He was staring a hole through me. When he approached me, he asked me if I were carrying any kind of live plant or animal with me. I told him no. He proceeded to ask me the same question again, but this time his wording was a little different, although it was still the same question. I answered, "No sir" again. I was so sure that I did not have anything illegal with me. I was also positive I had left the leftover fruit at the hotel in the garbage can. I wondered if they had found it or figured out that I had brought it with me on the way to Cancun.

Oh my goodness! What should I do? Maybe I'm just now going to get into big trouble for the fruit, I thought. I felt sick! My heart started beating very fast as I answered "no sir" again to the security officer. Then he asked, "What about the bird?" I looked at him with what must have been a startled look on my face and asked, "What bird?" He said, "The bird you are carrying with you."

Thank God, I instantly remembered the ceramic bird that I had bought for a souvenir in Cancun to take home with me. "Oh my!" I blurted out. I started laughing, but I was sure the man did not care for my humor. He wasn't smiling. I told him the bird that I had listed on my customs form was not a real live bird. He asked me if I were certain about that. I told him yes, that I was very sure, as I explained to him where I had purchased it. I thought I saw a very small grin on his face, as he told me to proceed ahead through the line. "Man!" I whispered to myself. "This trip is going to get the best of me yet." All I had on my mind now was getting back home safely.

Clark and I still had to go through the customs line. I couldn't believe all this was happening to me, and I couldn't wait for it to be over. It was finally my turn to go through the blinking lights when I got stopped again for a random search. It seemed like it took forever for them to check my entire luggage. I was sure they were looking at me with disbelief on their faces concerning all the clothing and shoes I had taken on the trip.

There was something in one of my suitcases that the authorities kept x-raying. It was one of my souvenirs that I had wrapped with some of my clothing. The clothing had kept the x-ray from being clear to them, they said. They told me to wrap the items in newspaper the next time so they could see them plainly. When everything was finally approved, I couldn't help but wonder if I would ever get back home. The rest of the flight went okay except that I was so exhausted again from the mega-luggage I had to deal with once more. *The cab driver is exhausted, too,* I thought to myself as I watched him put my luggage into the car at the airport. Even though I tipped him well, I kept thinking he would never want to give me a ride again because of the huge amount of weight he had to lift into the cab.

I had learned some huge lessons concerning our trip: do not overpack when I travel; do not wrap my breakable souvenirs with my clothing; watch closely what I write down on the customs form; do not drink alcohol before I fly; and, last but not least, leave my water and fruit at home.

Oh! By the way, I did get an upset stomach the day I arrived home, and the sickness lasted a couple of weeks. My doctor guessed that my illness may have been caused from brushing my teeth or eating the fruit in Mexico, because of the water I was not accustomed to. The only good thing that came from that incident was I lost five pounds, which didn't hurt me. I needed to lose it.

With all things considered, I had a great time in Cancun. I'm sure I would do it all over again, but I can't stress enough that I'd do a lot of it differently the next time. This was one vacation, though, that leaves me with nothing else to say but, **"What a trip!"**

The Deceitful Seed

Bless your food before you eat,
And ask to never be deceived.

D.J. DeSai

Several years ago, I remember wishing I could learn a few lessons from some of the gardeners who had green thumbs. Springtime was drawing near, and I found myself desiring their knowledge, and wanting to master their skill growing fresh veggies and fruits.

I had lived in the country until I was twelve years old, but I was too young then to have wanted, cared, or even longed to get my hands dirty on the farm. Gardening had been the last thing on my mind. Also, being blessed with three loving brothers, I had not been appointed as one of the helping hands when it came to the everyday outdoor chores.

When I turned thirty-three years old, I found myself missing an artistry that only some of that good old-fashioned practice may have taught me. Sad to say, I had gone through a divorce then too, so I was on my own for the first time in my life while raising two small children. I decided it was time for me to learn a little bit more about my country roots because, again, I wanted to grow my own garden. I started skimming through some home and garden books, and reading material I thought would be beneficial for learning to produce my own food from seed. Spring had arrived, so it would soon be time to start my planting.

A few days later, an elderly man named Perry, who worked with me, gave me some gardening advice. He also gave me an envelope filled with okra seed. A few days prior, I had told him how much I loved fried okra, so Perry had not forgotten it. He had been gardening for years, so it made him feel good to be a part of my new hobby, since he had such a love for it, too. I was very thankful for the okra seed Perry had brought me, and for every piece of information he had given me. I wanted my first garden to be a success. I was also hoping I would be able to grow enough food to give away to friends, family, and neighbors. It made me feel good to do things for other people.

First, I would need a rotor tiller to dig up the dirt in my back yard. I was more than excited when Perry volunteered to bring his tiller over and do that for me. I was also so grateful for his time and service that I promised him a big bag of tomatoes when my harvest was ready for picking. He laughed at me, glad that I had found a piece of the same happiness he had been carrying around with him for so many years.

After Perry tilled my ground, I decided to set out twenty tomato plants, fifteen pepper plants, a couple rows of corn, and some green beans. I carefully picked out where I wanted my veggies to go, while remembering to save enough room for my okra seed. After everything had been put in the ground and watered, I stood back and proudly gazed at my beautifully planted garden. I was pleased with it. Now, I was praying for a good rain.

A couple of days later, my prayers were answered. It rained steady for two straight days. I thanked God! My crop was looking good, and I couldn't wait to see my plants bloom. A few weeks later I was blessed with that, too. The plants were spreading out all over the place. I loved going to work and giving Perry and my other co-workers my progress report. They thought it was great that I was taking such an interest in gardening and, of course, they were all hoping for some fresh veggies from my garden.

A few more weeks went by when my crop finally arrived. I went out and picked several tomatoes, a bowl of green beans, and some fresh okra. I carried the food into the house, and washed it. I decided nothing would taste any better than a bowl of green beans cooked with some potatoes, onion, and ham. I also cut the four pieces of okra into several small pieces. Then I floured each one before I deep fried them in olive oil. I couldn't wait to feed my children some fresh food from my own garden. I knew this would be so much healthier for them, and I wanted them to have the best of nourishment. *I should have done this a long time ago,* I thought to myself. I couldn't help but smile as I filled the three plates with homemade food before setting them on the table.

My son, Jake, was nine years old, and my daughter, Mindy, was seven. Both children sat there at the kitchen table and stared at the food on their plates before turning their noses up in the air. They had disappointed looks on their faces as I said the blessings. I knew that after they had tasted their food, they would change their minds and not care about the way it looked or smelled. "It will be delicious," I told them. My two children slowly picked at the food on their plates before getting enough nerve to actually taste of it. I noticed they had not even given the okra a pick with their forks. I politely asked them to give it a try, but they both shook their heads, no.

While sitting there loving the taste of my fresh food, I was becoming slightly disappointed with my little ones because I felt sure they would like my food if they would just give it a fair chance. They still continued to tell me there was no way they wanted to try the nasty okra. They told me it had an ugly look. I raised my voice to them feeling a touch of anger rising up in me. I didn't want to get upset with them, but I only wanted them to experience the taste of my home grown food. I insisted they both take a big bite of the okra, quickly reminding them of all the children in the world who were less fortunate than they were when it came to having enough food to eat. I watched patiently as each one of my children poked their forks into a piece of the okra and hesitatingly put it into their mouths. They reluctantly chewed it up for what seemed like twenty minutes before they spit it out.

Trying to understand, I was still losing my patience with them. I knew they were just being picky. I told them they could be excused from the table, but they would not get dessert because they had not made a very good effort to finish their dinner. Actually, they had hardly eaten a thing. *Oh well. Maybe the next time,* I thought, *but I will definitely not give in to them concerning dessert. They need to know and appreciate the time I spent growing the garden, and also the fact that they have been blessed with fresh food to eat,* I reminded myself. I had hoped they would get hungry later and ask me for some more veggies, but this did not happen. They fell asleep shortly after dinner.

The next day I went to work with several bags of my home grown tomatoes and peppers. Each person was so appreciate of my kindness, and they bragged on my food all day long. Their compliments were worth every minute I had spent in the garden.

As the days grew hotter and hotter, I grew more tired of going out and hoeing my garden. I started letting it go, although I was concerned that my food would be snuffed out from all the weeds. I hated to see it go to waste, but I did get lazy.

One day my mother-in-law, Beth, stopped by to visit us. Before she left, I gave her some tomatoes to take home with her while telling her to go out to the garden and pick some okra for herself. I told her it looked as though it may be growing wild out there. The okra was spreading out all over the place.

Beth walked out to the garden and, much to my surprise, I heard her yell out, "Child, this is not okra, this is milkweed!" "Oh my God!" I prayed. "Are you sure?" I asked her. Beth said, "Yes, Dory, this is definitely milkweed." I told her that I had fed the milkweed to my children for dinner while thinking it was okra that I had planted. I had also eaten it myself. Beth told me I was probably lucky that we all had not gotten sick. I asked her if the milkweed was poisonous. She said, "No, Dory, I don't think so, but it can't be too healthy," as she laughed out loud.

Suddenly, I was so ashamed and embarrassed. I told Beth it was probably time for me to give up my gardening. She agreed with my suggestion at first, but then she told me that okra looks somewhat like milkweed, but I should have known the difference. I had not known the difference, obviously, or I would not have eaten it nor would I have fed it to my two children. I felt like a careless mother.

Needless to say, Beth turned down the okra offer, but I decided to keep gardening. I would just do it differently the next time. Since the milkweed and the okra are somewhat familiar in size, shape, and color, I figured I'd just stick to growing tomatoes and peppers. I could not believe I had eaten milkweed, because it had tasted great. Thankfully, I recalled my children spitting it back out of their mouths onto their plates.

A few weeks later, an article was printed in the daily newspaper, making me feel a little better. The author of the story had researched milkweed saying it is very high in calcium, and also safe to eat. I wondered if I might be "on to something" that may turn out to be a healthy, eatable veggie someday.

Nevertheless, I apologized to my children for trying to make them eat the milkweed. I told them I was so sorry that I had made such a huge mistake, while they laughed out loud at their dear mother. They thought the ordeal was so funny, but it also gave them an excuse for not wanting to eat all their veggies from that day forward. They would always ask me if I was certain they were really eating what I told them it was. Their teasing with me did nothing more than put a big smile on my face. I was so glad we could all joke around about it.

Yes, I had definitely been taught a good lesson, and thank God I have always made it a habit of asking the Lord to bless our food before each meal. I have also made a new vow to myself to always look for **"the deceitful seed."**

My Baby

Ever since Baby became my best friend,
I've longed to protect him until the end.

D.J. DeSai

When I found out my daddy was dying, I didn't want to believe it. I felt as though I needed him in my life more than ever then. The two of us had not had a very solid relationship while I was growing up, but a couple of years before he had gotten sick, we started getting closer. We found ourselves communicating in a healthy way for the first time so needless to say, I wasn't ready to accept the fact that I would have to give him up so soon.

One night my boyfriend, Chevy, came over to visit with me. It was the night before Easter Sunday, and he had brought me a gift. He handed me a little basket, and when I removed the blanket lying on top of it, I was so surprised. Inside was the cutest little apricot toy poodle lying sound asleep. "Happy Easter, Dory!" Chevy said. "Oh, thank you!" I said with excitement in my voice. The puppy was only a few weeks old, Chevy said, and I fell in love with him right away. He fit perfectly in the palm of my hand, and I loved holding him close to me, especially during the time of my dad's illness. My puppy gave me comfort. "What a wonderful gift!" I told Chevy.

At that time in my life, I wouldn't have thought I needed a dog. I wonder now how I managed without him. He kissed my face each time a tear fell from my eyes, making me feel as though he were mourning my dad's illness, just as I was.

Everywhere I would go, I would take my toy poodle with me. People would walk up to me, rub him, and talk baby talk to him while calling him

Baby. This must have happened at least one hundred times before I finally decided that there was no other name for my puppy but "Baby."

I wouldn't have taken a million dollars for Baby after holding him so close to me those first few days. I would rock him in my arms until he would go to sleep. I could hear every heartbeat and breath he would take. It made me feel so much better just having him near me, while feeling an overwhelming emptiness inside me, knowing I was losing my dad.

A few weeks later, my dad died as he was expected to, and I thought I would die too, right there with him. I may have mourned myself to death if it had not been for Baby. He was just what I needed at that time in my life, and I thanked my boyfriend Chevy again for giving him to me.

I grew closer and closer to Baby as he grew from a puppy to a dog. At full growth, he was still a very small toy poodle. He loved for me to cuddle and play with him. I taught him a lot of tricks because he was very smart and easy to train.

Mandy, my teenage daughter had grown fond of Baby, too. One day I came home from work to find her holding him. Mandy said Baby had been acting tired and she was sure he wasn't feeling well. We both kept an eye on our poodle for the next few days and when he didn't seem to be getting any better, we took him to the vet. Baby was not eating much if anything at all, and his breath smelled rank. The vet said he had a virus, so he gave me some antibiotics to give to him for the next several days.

A few more days passed by, and Baby was only getting worse. He would whine and just lie there looking helpless. He had no energy and everyone was getting more worried. He had completely quit eating and I had noticed he had not had a bowel movement at all. I took him back to the same vet before he had finished taking his medicine because I wondered if my dog had been misdiagnosed. The vet looked at Baby again and said he was still sick with the same virus. He told me that I needed to finish giving him the antibiotics. He also said for everyone to let him rest, and that he should be fine in a few days. I reluctantly took his word again. I took Baby back home, but something inside me was telling me the vet was wrong. I didn't know what else to do, though.

I waited another couple of days, but Baby still continued to get worse instead of better. I looked at him one night and cried as I held him close to me. I told Mandy and Chevy that I just knew my dog was dying. I told them that if someone didn't do something soon, Baby would not be around much longer. We all decided we should take Baby somewhere else for a second opinion. It was getting late in the day, so we had to hurry. We hoped and prayed we could find someone still open who would see him.

Chevy called and talked to another vet that night. The vet recommended that we call another vet named Dr. Yang. He said Dr. Yang was a Chinese vet and his office stayed open all night. He also told Chevy that he was very experienced. Chevy didn't waste any time calling Dr. Yang's office. The assistant who answered the phone told Chevy to bring Baby in immediately. I held Baby in my arms as we hurriedly drove to the office. After we arrived, Dr. Yang examined Baby, checking all his vital signs. Then he pushed on his stomach with a little force. Baby growled like he could have bitten someone's head off. I would have thought that Dr. Yang was torturing him, but this reaction told the vet exactly what Baby's problem was.

Dr. Yang said that Baby had eaten something that was still lodged in his stomach, and he would have to operate on him to remove it. Otherwise, Baby would definitely be dead by the following morning. He went on to say that there was only a fifty percent chance he would live anyway because he was so weak. The vet apologized, saying the poodle may not be strong enough to survive the surgery. He told us that he could not and would not promise us anything, but he would do all that he could do to save our dog.

"Oh my God!" I cried out to Jesus. I was so frightened and upset that I might lose Baby. I had come to love him so very much. He was only three years old, and I had grown so attached to him. He had become part of the family. My children were also crazy about Baby, especially Mandy. Mandy still lived at home with me, and she had been taking care of the dog while I worked.

Dr. Yang went on to explain to us why Baby's breath was so rank. He said our dog had not had a bowel movement because of what was lodged in his intestines. "Whatever this is has been blocking everything," the vet said. "Therefore, the only means of getting rid of his waste is through his mouth." As Dr. Yang continued to talk, the thought of everything he was saying really made sense, but it grossed us out, too. *No wonder Baby has been so sick!* I thought. *Why hadn't the other vet figured this out?* I kept asking myself. We were all so upset with ourselves for not getting a second opinion sooner. Now, it may be too late.

When Dr. Yang said he needed to go ahead and operate on Baby, he told all of us to go on home. He said he would call us after the surgery was over. He said the procedure would only take a couple of hours, but it would take a couple of days before he would know if our dog would make it or not. I held Baby in my arms for as long as I could before we left to go home. I told him I'd be right back and that I loved him with all my heart. It felt like my heart was breaking in two as I left the vet's office that night.

I was beside myself on the way home. I was a nervous wreck. It was close to midnight when I finally got in bed. I knew I had to get up and go to work the next day, but I couldn't sleep. I kept tossing and turning, hoping and praying that Baby would make it through the surgery.

Finally, around four o'clock in the morning I couldn't stand it any longer. I got up and called Dr. Yang's office to see how Baby was. "Yippee!" I shouted. I felt so relieved when he told me that Baby had made it through the surgery. Again, Dr. Yang said the next couple of days would be very critical.

When I was getting ready to hang the phone up, Dr. Yang asked me if I were ready for the verdict concerning what Baby had swallowed. I was surprised. I had forgotten all about that part while concentrating on Baby's survival. I told the vet I could take any kind of news as long as he would be okay. Dr. Yang went on to tell me that our dog had swallowed two used tampons. He said that one of them had been lodged in the front of his small intestines and the other in his stomach. The tampons had expanded after he had swallowed them so they couldn't go anywhere else but where he had found them. He told me that if I had not brought Baby in when I did, he would not have made it through the night. I thanked him and told him I had thought the same thing myself. This was the reason why I had brought him in. "I knew my dog was near death," I told him.

After I hung the phone up, I wondered where in the world Baby had gotten the used tampons and why he had eaten them. The very thought of him swallowing something so nasty made me feel sick, along with the thought of his bad breath. *Who in the world would think a dog would eat something like that?* I asked myself. It seemed absurd.

Mandy had never made it a habit of putting the lid on the garbage can in her bedroom, so Baby must have gotten into it while we were away from home. I didn't want to give my daughter any bad feelings concerning Baby's illness and surgery, so I decided not to throw blame to her. I did tell Mandy, though, what the vet had said about the tampons. I could tell by the look on her face that she was feeling guilty enough. Nothing else really needed to be said. It would be a good lesson learned.

The next morning I couldn't wait to go in to see Baby. Dr. Yang suggested I only stay for a minute. He said he wanted to give my dog the incentive to live by allowing him to see me, but he didn't want to tire him out too much. He said he was so weak from the sickness and the surgery. He said that all of it had really taken its toll on his fatigued little body. Dr. Yang was still worried that Baby might not make it, so, needless to say, I was even more worried.

When I went in to see him, he was just lying there looking so pitiful. All I could do was stand there and cry. He was trying to bark at me but there was no sound coming out of his mouth. He was too weak. Dr. Yang told me to leave the room quickly, because he didn't want Baby to get too excited or upset. I did as the vet told me to do, although I hated leaving him to go to work that day. Yes, it seemed like the longest day of my life. I could not concentrate on anything else but worrying about my sweet dog and praying he would be okay. I couldn't wait to go back over to see him. I was so anxious and scared all at the same time.

As soon as I left work that day, I headed straight for the vet's office. Dr. Yang said I could go in to see him again, but he still thought it best I stay for only a few minutes. Again, Baby just lay there. He slowly tried to work his body forward to get closer to me but he was still too weak to move much. It was so sad to see him looking like that. I decided to go on and leave so Baby could rest. It hurt me so badly, because we still didn't know if he would make it or not. Dr. Yang did tell me if he lived through one more night, he would most likely be out of the danger zone.

Again, I didn't sleep well that night. When I awoke, I couldn't wait to get ready to go see my dog. As soon as I walked into the vet's office, Dr. Yang greeted me with a smile on his face. I was sure that what he was going to tell me was all good. Sure enough, he told me he thought Baby would be okay. He said he wanted to get him out of the lighted cage to see if he could stand up on top of the table by himself. I waited.

When the vet brought my dog out, I could hardly see the two bandages on his belly. He was standing up and the bandages were hidden. When Dr. Yang stood him up on the table next to me, Baby moved as close to me as he could. I heard him moan softly as he slowly and carefully turned his whole body around. It was almost as if he wanted to make sure I could see his incisions. I couldn't believe that a dog as smart as Baby could have eaten something so nasty. "Why did he eat those tampons?" I asked Dr. Yang. Instead of answering my question, he asked me if we had been away from home for long periods of time, leaving Baby alone. I told him yes, we had. I told him that sometimes we have to be away from home for work related reasons. The vet said that oftentimes when pets are left alone, they start missing and grieving their owners. He said their loneliness causes them to look for odors from their masters. They usually look for items that they have touched or worn. He went on to say that sometimes pets will go as far as eating those things. "This makes them feel closer to their loved ones, since they are missing them and longing to be with them," he said. He also said pets do not know how nasty a dirty sock or a used tampon is. He went on to say that this is a very natural thing for them to do and it happens quite often. He told me not to take it personally but only to be more careful. I knew that in the future we would have to be very cautious as to what we left out and uncovered. I also knew that what I had previously heard about a dog's mouth being cleaner than a human's mouth could not be true. *I'll never believe that story again. How disgusting!* I thought.

Thank God, though, I had followed my gut feeling that night we took Baby to see Dr. Yang. I had been so sure that he would not make it and I was right about that. If we hadn't taken him to the vet when we did, he would have died. Dr Yang had confirmed that.

What I learned concerning that entire ordeal is this. Do not leave anything lying around for pets to eat unless you want them to eat it. When you have a sick pet, you should always get a second opinion because it is often required. Sick people get second opinions from their doctors all the time, so our pets should be worth this much, too.

My decision had saved my dog's life and I was so very thankful to leave the vet's office that day and to be able to go home with **"my Baby."**

Baby died on July 12th, 2006. A couple of days before his death, he developed a cough so I took him to the vet's office thinking he only had a cold. He died in my arms right there in the office. He was ten years old. The vet said that Baby had developed a disease called congestive heart failure. His heart had just given out at that very moment. I stood there in disbelief while crying my eyes out, patting and caressing my Baby who had gone home to Doggie Heaven.

Before I left the office, the vet talked me into cremating Baby. He thought this would be best, and I agreed, while not really knowing what I was doing. I was in a state of shock as I left the office. Yes, I had just left Baby lying there on the table. I was too hurt to pick him up and take him home to bury him.

I went on home and cried myself to sleep that night. I could not believe my Baby was really gone. It had happened so suddenly. I didn't even know he was sick until the day before I took him to the vet. Needless to say, it was a very restless night.

The next morning I woke up and wondered where my dog was. *Have they cremated him yet?* I wondered. I called the vet's office to tell them I wanted to pick Baby up and bring him home. There was no answer. "Oh my goodness!" I cried. I panicked! *What have they done with Baby?* I kept asking myself. I remembered telling the vet it was okay to cremate him. I vaguely recalled their saying they would put him with several other dogs when they performed the procedure. *Oh no!* I thought. *I want my dog back.* I didn't want him to be cremated with other dogs. I looked in the phone book and wondered where Baby was. I started calling every animal cremation place in the state. No one had seen or heard of Baby. I was beside myself! My dog was nowhere to be found. *Where in the world can my Baby be?* I wondered.

A few hours later, after calling everyone I could find in the phone book, I tried the vet's office again. Finally, someone answered. The vet told me that Baby had been stored in the freezer, awaiting someone to pick him up to take him to be cremated. I asked him if my dog was in the freezer alone. He told me to hold on. He said he would go check to see exactly where he was. A few minutes later he came back and told me that Baby was lying on top of the other dogs. He tried to console me by telling me that Baby was the "cream of the crop." I told him I was coming to pick him up. The vet was quick to tell me that he thought I was making a huge mistake. He said he didn't think I should see my dog looking the way he looked, and that I should remember him the way he was the last time I saw him.

I thought about it for a minute and decided he was probably right. I told the vet that I didn't want Baby to be cremated with other dogs. He said he understood and he would arrange that request for me. I had to pay the difference in the price, of course, but the money didn't matter. I wanted only Baby's ashes.

A few days later, I received a call to pick up Baby's remains. Before I left the parking lot with his ashes in the tin vase, I looked at the certificate they had filled out. "Oh no!" I gasped. The day of Baby's death was not recorded correctly on the form.

Baby had died on July 12th and they had typed July 13th on the paper. *I wonder if the ashes are really Baby's indeed,* I thought to myself. I was so upset! I called the office while I was still in the parking lot and they looked up the information on the computer. The assistant came back to the phone and told me that her co-worker had only recorded the date wrong, and they were so sorry for the typo they had made. She tried to convince me that there was no mistake concerning my dog's identity. Needless to say, I wondered if this were the truth. I still wonder today if the ashes in my tin vase really and truly belong to **"my Baby."**

Picked Three, Bet Two, 'n' Won Five

Thank God for each and every awesome day,
And thank Him for blessings He sends our way.

D.J. DeSai

When we wake up each morning, we never know what the day may bring. We all hope for the very best, but occasionally it doesn't turn out that way. Each time I thank God for an extraordinary day, though, I feel the need to share it with others. I hope you'll enjoy reading about one of my most financially blessed days. And may the Lord bless you this much when you need it the most, just as I did then.

I definitely do not encourage gambling whatsoever. I don't see anything wrong with it, though, if it is done in moderation. If it's fun, it's fun. If it isn't fun, it's probably not healthy, and may very well hurt you or someone you love.

A good friend of mine named Ned stopped by my house one day to visit. It was my day off from work and Ned knew this. He asked me if I would like to go to the race track with him. I told him I had too many things on my plate to do that day, so I'd better not. Ned had a racing program with him that he had picked up earlier at a nearby store. He asked me if I wanted to place a bet. He told me he would get me a ticket if I wanted him to. I shook my head, no. I couldn't afford to bet. I had too many bills looking at me, and I was wondering how in the world I would pay them. I also needed a new roof on my home, too. I had been praying, asking God to help me, and I believed he would.

I have never made it a habit of gambling, although I have always enjoyed being around the race horses. I grew up with family members and friends who have always been involved in the horse business, so sometimes I will bet a couple of dollars just for the fun of it.

While glancing at Ned's racing program for just a quick moment, I decided it might be fun to make a little bet. Immediately, I noticed three races in a row with horses' names listed that were related to music. I love music so I told Ned I liked all three names of those particular horses. One horse's name was Sweet Melody, one was Guitar Man, and the other name was Piano Notes. I asked my friend if he would get me a two-dollar pick-three bet on those three races using those three horses' names. The pick-three bet meant that all three horses of each race had to win in order for me to win. Ned told me that my two-dollar pick-three bet was probably as good a bet as any, and he would be more than glad to get the ticket for me since he was going anyway. I circled all three horses I had picked, and then gave Ned the two dollars for my bet.

Ned called me from the race track after the last of the pick-three races had run. With much excitement in his voice, he yelled, "Dory, you won!" "Oh, thank you so much," I told Ned, while thanking God, too, and thinking that I may have won twenty or thirty dollars. I was busy doing laundry, and I was getting ready to hang the phone up when I heard Ned say, "Wait a minute, Dory. I'm bringing the winning ticket to you." I thanked him again, and I was getting ready to hang the phone up for the second time when he yelled out, "Don't you want to know how much your pick-three ticket is worth?" There was a brief silence before I heard Ned say, "All three of your horse picks that pertained to music won, and your two-dollar pick-three ticket is worth over five thousand dollars!" "Oh my God!" I shouted out to the Lord. I thanked Jesus and Ned for the largest financial blessing I had ever encountered in my entire life. I was more than excited. I could not believe I had won five thousand dollars by only betting two dollars. I was overwhelmed with emotion. Ned was excited for me, too.

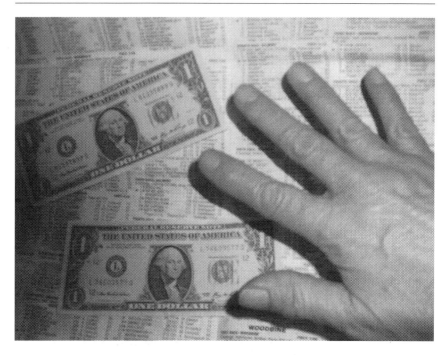

Of course, I tipped Ned as much as he would allow me to after I cashed my ticket the next day. I was so very thankful for the money, and it couldn't have come at a better time in my life. I was struggling while raising my two children. Again, I was in need of many things and I had been praying and wondering how in the world I would come up with the money. *Thank God! I finally have as much as I need,* I thought. I was also so grateful that Ned had stopped by that day. If it were not for my friend and my feeling the music so to speak, I certainly would not have **"picked three, bet two, 'n' won five."**

Seven Days in a Bucket

Fix it if it's broken or be quick to call a pro,
When it involves a toilet and you really have to go.

D.J. DeSai

One lesson that I have been taught in the past is that sometimes I need a plan A, a plan B, and maybe a plan C. It can't hurt to have alternative back-up methods for security purposes. I am also a firm believer in "if first you don't succeed, then try, try again." Don't forget to try something different the next time, though, if the same arrangement continues to fail over and over again. This story is an illustration, proving all the above to be true.

Summer was drawing near, and spring break at school had finally arrived for my two children. On a whim, I decided to take off from work for a week to spend some quality time with my two little ones. I couldn't really afford to take them on a trip, so I was hoping I could show them a little fun at home to make up for it. We could go somewhere some other time, hopefully. My children were six and eight years old then, and so full of energy. Needless to say, I knew the next several days would be a very busy time for me, but I was actually looking forward to it. I was sure there would be enough time for rest and relaxation, too.

Around the middle of the week, I noticed that my toilet was flushing abnormally. I had been using a plunger for a couple of days, because the water had been draining very slowly. Now it was starting to back up. I did not have the first clue as to what was going on. I knew I couldn't keep plunging the commode after every flush, feeling certain it would eventually overflow and ruin my floor. I told my children I was going to have to call a plumber, while silently thinking I could not really afford one.

Before I picked up the phone to call for help, my eight-year-old son, Jake, finally spoke up and told me what he thought the problem was. He said he had accidentally flushed the plastic toilet paper holder and this could be the reason why the water wasn't going down. *Oh yes,* I thought to myself. "This could surely cause a problem," I told my son. Jake went on to say that the holder had fallen into the commode while he was trying to put a new toilet paper roll on. He told me he had forgotten to get the holder out before he flushed the toilet. He also said, "I'm sorry, Mommy," so how could I be upset with him? He didn't mean to do it, and besides, I did not think it was a big deal. I had wondered where my plastic holder had gone to, but I'd been too busy to really dwell on it. *Oh well. Accidents happen,* I thought to myself. I told Jake we would get the holder out one way or another.

I went into the bedroom and grabbed a wire coat hanger from the closet. I twisted the hanger several times while trying to straighten it out the best I could. Then I wiggled it upwards through the hole as far as I could to try and grasp the toilet paper holder. I must have tried this technique for a couple of hours, having no luck. I was growing tired. The toilet was still stopped up, so I knew the holder must still be lodged inside the commode somewhere.

Feeling aggravated, I decided to take a break when I heard my phone ringing. I answered it to hear my friend Molly on the other line. I explained to Molly what I'd been doing. She told me that she would be glad to come over and help me out if I wanted her to. She knew my funds had been running low since my husband and I had split up. I told her it was so sweet of her to volunteer her time and thanked her. I went on to tell Molly that I was going to work with my commode a little longer, and if I couldn't fix it, I may call on her for help later.

For the next few minutes, I continued to work with the wire hanger, but still, I had no luck. I wondered what in the world had happened to make matters worse because now it was impossible for me to even flush the toilet while using the plunger. The water had started over-flowing in the bathroom floor, so I had to turn off the valve until it finally drained. I was getting discouraged and losing patience. My children were also pleading desperately for me to let them use the restroom, but now it was completely out of order.

Naturally, the children continued to whine, so I ran outside and grabbed a bucket so we would all have something to use while the commode was down. After the children had relieved themselves, they started laughing and making fun of the bucket, but I reminded them that when I was their age, my family and I had to use an outdoor toilet twenty-four-seven. I explained to them that when it got too cold to go outside, a bucket sure did come in handy. The kids thought my comment was so funny.

As I stood in the hallway, and all out of ideas concerning fixing the toilet, I decided to call Molly back. After a couple of rings, she answered. Molly told me she was cooking dinner, but she would come over early the next morning to help me. I thanked her as we hung up the phones.

Before my children went to bed, I reminded them that they would have to continue using the bucket for the night. Again, they laughed at the bucket, but I was sure their laughing was not as intense as it was before. There was definitely nothing funny about the stopped-up situation. It had become somewhat annoying.

The next morning Molly called and said she'd be over in a little while. Later that afternoon, she walked into my house with nothing in her hand but a wire hanger. I told her that I had already tried that same method, but it had not worked. "As a matter of fact, using the hanger has only made things worse," I told her. Molly laughingly told me that the hanger she had was different from mine, and I should go into the other room, chill out, and let her fix the problem. She sounded sure she could un-clog my commode, so I certainly did not want to get in her way. Before I left Molly alone in the bathroom, I showed her where the bucket was located, just in case she needed to use it. She rolled her eyes and shook her head, while laughing at my bucket, too.

A couple more hours went by and, sad to say, Molly had no luck unclogging the toilet either. She had not improved the problem any more than I had. By this time, it was starting to get dark outside and I was sure it was too late to call a plumber. No doubt, we were all getting more and more anxious about getting the commode fixed. Jake kept apologizing to me about flushing the toilet paper holder, while I kept reminding my son not to worry. I assured him we would get it fixed soon.

Around dinner time, Molly said she needed to go home. I thanked her for spending so much of her time trying to help. She told me she'd be back over the next morning with some different tools, but I told her not to worry about it because I was ready to bite the bullet and call a plumber. Molly insisted that I not call a plumber. She told me that she had unclogged plenty of commodes in the past, and she was very confident that she could fix it if she had the right tools. I argued with her, but she would not give up. I finally decided to give my friend one more chance so needless to say, we all went to bed again that night toilet-less, and still using a bucket.

Gee! Day three in a bucket had arrived and everyone woke up complaining and heading straight for a bad mood. Not having a toilet had become a huge nuisance. *Surely we will get it unclogged today,* I hoped. *If not, I will definitely call for professional help. I'll have no other choice no matter what the cost,* I thought.

Molly called me early that morning to say she would be over soon with her handyman tools. I breathed a sigh of relief, telling her that I would be tickled pink when we were able to use our restroom again. She laughed and said she knew the tools would work, and she apologized to me for not bringing them with her the afternoon before. I was very thankful that I had someone who was volunteering to help me out. *Maybe I won't have to clean out my checking account by having to pay a plumber after all,* I thought to myself.

A little while later, Molly walked in my house carrying a big tool box. I laughed at her, telling her I was sure she could perform a man's job any day with the various tools she had. As the two of us headed for the bathroom, I told my friend I would leave her alone while she worked. Yes, I would let Molly do her thing because my expertise was definitely not in the home maintenance department. I knew how to use a hammer and a screwdriver, but that was about it.

As I listened closely from the basement, I heard the toilet flushing several times while I was doing laundry. I wondered if Molly was making any progress. I had just removed some clothes from the dryer when all of a sudden I saw mega water gushing down from the upstairs floor of the bathroom. It was seeping through the ceiling of the basement, soaking all my clean clothes. I knew it was the water from the toilet seeping from the floor so I was sure I would have to rewash all of my soiled clothing. Everything was a mess! I yelled as loudly as I could, telling Molly to turn the valve off.

For the next few minutes, the water continued to flow steadily through the two-by-fours on the basement's ceiling. *Wow! This is certainly not good for the wood,* I thought to myself. Molly had turned the valve off but it took a couple of minutes for all the water to stop draining. "Gee! What a mess!" I whispered to myself. I knew that she had tried her best to unclog the toilet, so I was trying my best to stay calm when I told her I was going to call someone else to fix the problem. Molly quickly agreed while saying, "Don't worry, Dory. I have a male friend that does this type of work on the side, and I will be more than glad to give him a call." I thanked Molly while asking her if he were a reputable plumber. She assured me that he would not only be a good repairman, but he would also be very reasonable when it came to the cost of the repairs. I told her that would be a tremendous blessing as I thanked her again.

The two of us talked about the plumbing problem for a few more minutes when suddenly, we both started laughing out loud, thinking of how we had both tried to fix the commode. We made a pact that we would never tell anyone else about our toilet excursion which had definitely not worked out.

Before Molly left, she called her handyman friend whose name was Seth. Seth was not at home, but his wife said he should be calling or coming home for lunch shortly. Seth's wife said she'd have him call Molly as soon as she heard from him. Molly thanked her hanging the phone up.

By this time, it was late in the afternoon so my children had already eaten lunch. Molly and I decided to eat too, as we waited for Seth to call. A little while later, Seth called back and said he would be more than glad to fix the toilet, but he would not be able to get to it until the next day. Needless to say, I was very disappointed. I didn't really want to wait another day, but I really didn't have a lot of money to spend either. I also knew if I were to call another plumber so late in the day, he probably couldn't come over until the next day anyway. I decided I'd better wait on Seth. Besides, Molly had reassured me that Seth would not charge me a lot of money since he was a good friend of hers. This was a very comforting thought for me. I was also very thankful that Molly had given up most of her afternoon to come over to assist me, even though it had not worked out.

Waking up the next morning and trying to survive day four in a bucket, I assured my children again that the toilet would be repaired soon. I had taken the week off from work and now I had only one more vacation day left. I really needed to get the plumbing problem fixed and out of the way. Everyone was getting so tired of using the bucket instead of the commode. It was also exhausting for me. I had to double bag the bucket every time someone had to go. Until now, I had not realized what a luxury the toilet had been. I was praying that today would be the day it would finally be fixed. I wondered if the Lord were trying to teach me some things, while I struggled through this dilemma.

That morning I cleaned the bathroom as best as I could, anticipating Seth's arrival soon. I waited patiently for most of the morning wondering why he had not shown up yet. Molly had told me he was a very busy man, but he had promised to arrive at my home before noon.

As the clock moved slowly, I started to worry. Anxiously, I decided to call Molly to ask her what she thought the problem might be. I reminded her that half the day was already gone and Seth had not arrived yet. Molly told me she would call Seth and then call me right back.

I waited patiently, wondering if I should go ahead and call another plumber. I quickly decided it would be best to respect Molly and wait a few more minutes. Thank God, it didn't take her long to call me back to tell me that Seth would be on his way as soon as he finished his next appointment. I teasingly told Molly that maybe I should call someone else just in case Seth didn't show up. There was a silence for a moment, and I sensed that she may be getting a little upset. Then I detected a little hurt in Molly's voice when she said, "Dory, I know Seth well, and he is a very dependable man, indeed." She assured me again that there was no need to worry, because Seth would be arriving at my home soon.

After Molly and I said our goodbyes, I hung the phone up and started dinner. Preparing our meal would be one less thing I'd have to do later. As time kept passing, I was starting to get very angry when I finally heard the doorbell ring. It was almost dinner time by then and I needed to start getting my children and myself ready for bed.

As soon as I answered the door, Seth apologized to me several times for taking so long to get to my home. He seemed to be a very nice man and I felt a little guilty for being so irritated with him. He immediately brought his tool box in, as I led him to the bathroom. I told him we were counting our days without a toilet and we were on day four. Seth laughed as I also told him we couldn't wait to get it fixed. He told me he understood my frustration and would have it repaired in a jiffy. "A jiffy" sounded like words spoken from heaven, and I smiled at him.

A few minutes later Seth came out of the bathroom with a worried look on his face. Needless to say, I became worried, too. He proceeded to gently break the bad news to me. I could feel my stomach getting upset as I listened closely to his words. He told me that he was going to have to take the toilet all the way up, because he could not unclog it with the snake he had brought. He said he was so sorry, because he would not be able to fix the toilet until he bought a new waxed toilet ring to put under it. He said he could not use the same one again after he took the commode up. Seth apologized to me for not having a new waxed ring with him, telling me that he normally carries them on his truck. He said he had run out of the rings and didn't know it. Of course, all the stores were closed by then. He went on to say that if he took the commode up to unclog it, and then put the toilet back down without a new waxed ring, the toilet would most likely leak afterwards. Seth said he wanted to do the job right. I really appreciated what he was saying, I told him, but I was greatly disappointed it could not be repaired that night.

Before Seth left, he assured me that the toilet would not be a problem to fix, and for me not to worry myself over it. He also told me he knew it was a very big deal not having a working commode, and apologized to me again for not having the proper equipment to fix it. He asked me if it would be okay if he came back the next day with a new waxed ring. I told him I had to work the next day, and I would not be home until six o'clock the next evening. Seth said the time did not matter to him if it didn't matter to me. I told him the only thing that mattered to me was getting my toilet fixed, and also what he was going to charge me. He told me that he would only charge for the price of the waxed seal ring that he needed to buy. He said that I had been so patient with him, and since I was a friend of Molly's, he would do the job free. I thanked him for that. He apologized again before he left.

I wondered what Seth would say if he only knew the truth. I had not been very patient at all since the entire toilet ordeal had started. I had been fussing to myself since the second day we had started using that awful plastic bucket. Oh well. I was not going to tell Seth anymore than I had to. All I knew was that I had to wait until the next day to get the commode fixed. Reluctantly, I went outside to wash the bucket out again, so it would be ready for use the next morning.

Because I had gone to bed that night so tired and stressed out, I must have forgotten to set the alarm clock because it didn't go off the next morning. Everyone overslept and everything was very hectic while the kids and I were running around trying to get ready. I had to empty and clean the bucket out after everyone, including myself, had used it. Yes, it was the fifth day in a bucket, but I was sure we would have a working toilet that night. I was thinking positive. "Yippee!" I shouted out loud. I was feeling very excited.

On my way to work that morning, the thought crossed my mind that I should have left Seth a hidden house key. *Maybe he can fix the toilet while I'm at work,* I thought. *I don't really know him very well though, but Molly knows him. Oh well. It probably doesn't matter much anyway. We'll be gone all day, so we won't need to use the toilet until we get home,* I told myself.

It certainly was a big blessing to go back to work and be able to use the restroom, in which the commode actually flushed. *Wow! I will try to never take one more thing for granted again,* I thought. *I will always try my best to appreciate everything in my life, because I feel like I have been living back in the fifties again, and this is not any fun at all.* I thought of my children staying with the sitter that day, and I was sure they felt the same way I did. They could finally use a commode that worked.

Soon, my work day was over and I headed for my car. As I rushed to the sitter's house to pick up my children, I couldn't help but smile. I wondered if they would even want to come back home with me after getting used to using a working toilet. When they got into the car, I was sure to tell them that our commode would definitely be fixed before we went to bed that night. They were so grateful, and so was I.

I rushed home to call Seth so he would not waste any time coming over. The phone rang; Seth answered it, and told me he would be there shortly, and we hung the phones up. *Praise God!* I thought to myself. My children and I started singing and dancing. We were so happy that we had something so special to look forward to. Maybe you could say it didn't take a lot to make the three of us happy, and it didn't, but getting the toilet fixed meant everything to us.

Seth rang the doorbell a few minutes later, and I was quick to let him in. "I have come prepared and equipped this time with everything I need," he said. He asked me if I would go down to the basement and turn off the main water valve so he could start his work. I told him I would, as he headed straight to the bathroom. *Ah! I finally feel relief. It will all be over soon,* I told myself.

After I got the children ready for bed, I walked into the bathroom to see what Seth was doing. I thought I might learn something. It had not taken him long at all to get the commode off of its waxed seal. "Wow! The hole is really clogged up with toilet tissue," I told him. Seth agreed, as he dug around for a minute before picking up the toilet paper holder and laying it in the garbage can. It had been lodged deep inside the hole, causing everything else to back up. Gee! It was hard to believe that something so small had caused such a huge problem. I was just so thankful to Seth for finally fixing it. He put the new waxed seal on, and then set the toilet back down on top of it.

At last, I felt like celebrating, but it was too late. I was too tired! Seth did a little caulking around the edges, and then gathered up his tools and walked back out to his truck. I followed him out and paid him for the waxed toilet seal he had given me a receipt for. I asked him if I needed to pay him for his services, but he assured me it was not necessary. I told him how thankful I was for all of his work as we said goodbye.

After I walked back into the house, the first thing I did was throw the bucket out in the back yard. What a wonderful feeling! Then I got ready for bed. I brushed my teeth, but before I called it a night, I couldn't wait to use my toilet. Seth had flushed it once before he left to make sure it was working and it was, thank God.

I walked into the bathroom and sat down on the commode. "Oh no!" I cried out. As soon as my bare feet hit the floor, I felt water. I looked down and couldn't believe my eyes. I saw water seeping out from under the commode. I wondered what in the world was going on now.

Feeling annoyed to the hilt, I got up and ran downstairs to the basement into the laundry room where the water had leaked before. There was another mess. I felt sick as I looked at the water all over my washer and dryer. The floor was completely soaked, too. I could still see the water dripping. I wondered what Seth had done wrong. *Why is this happening again?* I asked myself. *Seth must have put the waxed seal on wrong. I can't believe it! How long will this horrendous ordeal go on? I'm starting to think I have been cursed by someone or something. No one should have this much trouble with anything,* I thought. I felt so discouraged. I just wanted to scream. I could also feel my temper rising as I wondered if Seth knew anything at all about plumbing. It appeared he did not. I felt stupid, because I had trusted my friend Molly's judgment. I should have checked him out myself. Although I had not paid him anything, all I had really wanted was to have my toilet fixed. This nightmare had been going on for five long days. Money was not even an issue anymore. What was I going to do now? I was so distraught.

After I walked back outside to bring the bucket back in, I turned the water to the commode off. There was no sense in using it if we couldn't flush it. I decided that no matter what, I had to have this problem fixed soon, or I was sure to have a nervous break down.

Standing in the hallway, I wondered if I was making a mistake when I picked up the phone to call Seth. I was so desperate and there was no one else to call that late. He didn't live far from me, so I knew he was probably home already. I also wondered if the problem was something simple, and could be fixed immediately. Thankfully, I had calmed down some before the phone started to ring.

When Seth answered, I told him about the water problem. He said he thought everything was fine before he left. I told him I thought it was all good too, until I saw water gushing out onto the floor. He told me he would come back over the next morning before I left to go to work. I thanked him as we hung the phones up. All I had enough energy left to do was fall directly on my bed from being so tired and stressed out.

Before I fell asleep that night, I set my alarm clock an hour earlier than usual. I could not afford to be late for work. I knew it would take extra time for Seth to look at the toilet, so I tried to compensate for that. Gee! I could not believe I was preparing myself to wake up to day six without a toilet.

The next morning Seth arrived at the exact time he said he would. He went in, turned the water back on and flushed the toilet a couple of times to find out for himself what I had already told him. Oh no! Seth had only made another mess that I would have to clean up before I went to work. After he looked at all the water on the floor, he told me he was certain the toilet had a hair-line crack in it. He said it probably occurred while I was trying to unclog the toilet using one of my tools. He told me he was sure I would have to buy a new commode. He asked me if I wanted him to pick one up at the hardware store that day. He said he would come back over the following evening when I got home from work and install it for me. I asked Seth if I had another choice, but he said, no. He told me he had another job to finish and it would take all day. The next evening would be the soonest he could do it. Disappointedly, I told him to go ahead and buy the new toilet, and I would see him then. *What will one more day matter?* I silently wondered. Seth said okay, with little enthusiasm in his voice. Of course, he was getting as weary as I was concerning the toilet torment.

Unbelievable but true, my children and I were still toilet-less. The next morning was day seven in a bucket. *That's right! Day seven!* I thought to myself. I woke up tired, and I did not want to go to work. I did not feel good either, so I decided to call in sick. I wasn't lying. I really was feeling sickly. I was especially feeling terrible over this horrifying tribulation that would not go away. I decided I would take care of this problem today come hell or high water. I only hoped and prayed, though, that I would not see either hell or high water. I had definitely seen a lot of them both lately, and I was more than ready to kiss them goodbye forever.

I called Seth that morning to tell him I would be home all day if he could come over sooner than we had planned. I also told him I appreciated all that he was doing. He told me he couldn't believe all of this was happening concerning my commode. "Yes," I told Seth. "If it were not for bad luck, I'd have no luck at all." Seth and I both managed to laugh about my comment but I could tell he was getting as discouraged as I was by then. He had been working for free, and I was certain he was sorry he had even volunteered his services by now.

Seth called me around lunch time to tell me he had the new toilet on his truck. He said he would be right over. I did not have it in me to get excited over the new commode, so I just yawned, thanked him, and told him I'd be waiting for him.

Half an hour later he arrived. He came in and quickly removed the cracked toilet and waxed seal. Then he put the new waxed seal down, and, last but not least, he put the new toilet in. It was done! It was finished! Seth told me he wanted to turn the water back on and flush the toilet a few times to make sure everything was okay before he left this time. I told him that was the best idea I had heard in a long time.

Seth and I stood in the bathroom while he flushed the new toilet. "Oh no!" I screamed. After he had flushed the toilet twice, mega water started flooding the bathroom floor again. By then, all I could do was sit down and cry. The new toilet was leaking, too. After a few minutes, I got hold of myself and ran to the basement to see what was happening. It looked as though my home were flooding again. Water was running everywhere. Why was this happening? I did not understand plumbing, and I sure didn't understand why this problem could not be fixed.

I ran back up the steps and saw Seth standing there with his hands over his face. He told me he did not know what the problem could be. He said he had performed this same job many times before, but he had never had this kind of trouble before. I was starting to question his ability by then, but I was too upset to even talk about it. I told him I thought the best thing for me to do would be to call someone else. He told me he understood. I asked him if I owed him anything, and he gave me the receipt for the commode. He told me if there was a problem with it, I could take it back for an exchange or refund with my receipt. I paid him, and then he left.

Maybe I had offended Seth, but I did not know what else to do. I needed to get my toilet fixed, because I was off from work, and I was afraid to trust him again. Honestly, I doubted he even wanted to try fixing it again. Yes, I was sure that he was as aggravated and stressed out as I was by then.

As soon as Seth left, I called the hardware store where he had bought the new toilet. I talked to the manager explaining to him everything I had been through for the past seven days. The manager referred me to the plumbing department so I had to tell another man my toilet story. This time I was talking to someone who was an employee and also a plumber. The man put me on a phone hold for a few minutes. He told me *he* needed to talk to the manager about my problem.

A few minutes later, he returned to the phone and told me he was coming to my home with a new toilet and a new waxed ring. He told me that he would personally install my toilet for me at no charge. I was sure that both men felt very sorry for me after I had poured out my "oh my goodness" story to them. I thanked the man as we hung up the phones. I still couldn't help but believe that God was trying to teach me something very important. Maybe it was simply patience.

Alex, who was the plumber from the hardware store, arrived a couple of hours later with my new toilet. Within an hour he had it hooked up and working. "Oh my God! Thank you Jesus!" I shouted. The new toilet was wonderful! I must have ran up and down the basement steps ten times to check for water leaks while Alex stood there and watched me with a big grin on his face. He must have been thinking I was a crazy woman, but I couldn't believe it! There were no leaks anywhere, and I could flush my new toilet as many times as I wanted to. Alex said the new toilet that Seth had purchased for me at the hardware store was damaged. He said it had a manufacture's defect. "The commode he bought had a hairline crack," Alex told me. I explained to Alex that the hairline crack was the same problem I had with my first toilet. I quickly decided I owed Seth an apology. I told myself I would call him first thing the next morning. *Yes, I need to tell him I am sorry,* I thought to myself.

Before Alex left my home, he told me he would take the defective toilet with him, so the store could compensate for the new one he had brought to me. He did not charge me any money because I had already paid for the commode he was taking with him. Alex told me it was not my fault; therefore, he would not charge me for the labor involved either. I gave Alex a big hug before he walked out the door. He smiled at me and said, "I've never seen anyone so happy about a new toilet." I couldn't help but laugh out loud. "What can I say? I'm more than happy! I'm on cloud nine!" I told Alex.

Feeling so blessed that this crazy nightmare was finally over, I thanked the Lord. I never knew that my children and I could feel so wonderful concerning a working toilet. Yes, we've decided that our new commode is a better gift than any vacation we could have taken. We've also decided that we deserve the brand new toilet. Royally! Needless to say, we are very grateful, especially after knowing what it feels like to use the restroom for **"seven days in a bucket."**

What Goes Around Comes Around

Never say never, or you may eat those words,
And if so they may be a good lesson learned.

D.J. DeSai

We've all experienced some type of fear during our lives at one time or another. However, we don't always understand someone else's fear. It's also very easy to point our finger at someone when we have no clue as to what he or she may be going through. Accusations and judgments can backfire on us so quickly, biting us later on where it hurts.

Around the age of twelve, I moved with my family from the country to the big city. My parents had bought a large two-story home, and they assigned me one of the bedrooms upstairs. I loved the privacy. My three brothers were a little envious of me, because sometimes being an only daughter entitled me to certain privileges. One of those female rights meant me having a big bedroom all for myself.

My parents could not afford an air conditioner back then, and oftentimes it would get very hot inside the house, especially upstairs, and mainly during those dog days of July and August. All we were able to afford were fans to cool our home, but this didn't seem to help much.

One hot day during the month of August, I was looking inside my bedroom closet trying to find something cool to wear. Suddenly, my closet door accidentally closed shut on me. Previously, I had been having trouble with the door knob falling off, but I had forgotten to ask someone to fix it for me. I was sure there must have been a piece of it missing, but I was unable to repair it myself. I assumed my parents would have to buy a new door knob for me.

Consequently, at the same time the closet door closed behind me, the door knob fell off, too. "Oh my God!" I shouted. All I could do was pray. It was so dark inside the closet, and the heat was almost unbearable that day. It was at least one hundred degrees outside. My heart skipped a few beats from the panic attack I felt coming on when I realized there was no way I could open the door from the inside. Suddenly, I thought I was going to pass out from both fear and heat. I immediately started screaming at the top of my lungs, but unfortunately I wasn't loud enough. My voice could not scream above the rock and roll music that my three brothers were listening to that day. They had two gigantic speakers hooked up to their stereo, and I was quite sure the volume was turned up to the max. All I could hear was the noisy music playing, so needless to say, no one could hear my small faint screams from inside the small closet.

As I stood there in the hot and dark tiny space, I wiped the sweat and tears from my face. Then I jumped up and down, hoping my brothers would hear my feet tapping on the floor above them. It was no use! They could not hear me, and I was only making myself hotter. I said another prayer to Jesus. I was convinced that there was a God, but the more I hyperventilated, the more I wondered where he was. All I knew to do was to keep asking the Lord to help me. I wondered if hell were as hot as it was inside my closet. I hoped not!

I got down on my knees and used my hands to search for the door knob in the dark. I could not see anything. I could not find anything. It was useless! I was certain the door knob was on the other side of the door lying on the floor somewhere. All I could feel was the small hole in the door where the knob used to be. I was so scared and quite certain I might be running out of air to breathe. I felt so closed in. I wanted out of there so badly. Oh! How I longed for some cool air.

Finally the music ended, so I knew I had to act quickly between the small break of silence before the next song came on. I was so sure if there were any chance of my being saved, there was no time to waste. Aggressively, I put every ounce of energy into my next scream, hoping and praying that one of my three brothers would hear my desperate cry for help, and come and rescue me.

Soon the stereo started playing another song, so I lay down on the dark hardwood floor, deciding to just give up. Using the small amount of energy I had left was pointless. I was so tired and faint, and no one could hear my frail cry anyway. *Maybe someone will find me later, but it will probably be too late,* I hopelessly thought. I felt sure I would die soon.

Surprisingly, I heard a familiar voice calling out my name. I knew it was my brother Jimmy coming to save me from death. I was so thankful to hear his sweet voice, but for the next couple of minutes, I wondered if he were too late. I was so weak by then.

Jimmy yelled at me, as I yelled back at him with not much strength left in my voice. I told him I was locked in the closet and that I could not breathe very well. He told me he would be back in a minute, and to hold on. I wondered where Jimmy had gone, because I knew my parents were away, and they could not help him get me out. I was still full of worry, feeling my body fading fast, as the long drawn-out seconds turned into tormented minutes. I was trying to hold on as I waited for my brother to come back for me.

A couple of minutes later, Jimmy returned and immediately opened the closet door for me. I remember thinking he was my prince, and I would always be grateful to him. He had gone to the kitchen to get a butter knife. Then he used it to pry the door open for me. *What a gem Jim will always be in my eyes!* I thought.

Finally, I felt the somewhat cool air hit my face as Jimmy helped me out of the heated furnace I had been trapped in for what seemed like eternity. I could hardly stand up. I had to go lie down on my bed and rest for awhile after I had drunk a couple of glasses of cold water. Of course, my room was still hot, but not like the closet had been.

Later that day, as I was remembering what had happened to me, I couldn't help but cry. Being locked inside the closet had been a nightmare for me! I was sure my three brothers had worried about me that afternoon, because they kept the music turned down low. They also checked in on me every few minutes. I was so thankful for their concern, and more grateful than that to be out of that hot closet.

The next few years flew by, and needless to say, I had become very claustrophobic. I found myself always avoiding doors that might trap me inside. Of course, I was more than fearful of elevators. They gave me a closed-in feeling that the closet ordeal had given me, and I hated it. Usually, I felt okay about getting on an elevator if I had my cell phone with me. Oftentimes, though, if the elevator door did not open immediately, I would feel a panic attack coming on. There was nothing I could do to get over all the bad feelings, so I was forced to live with them.

One day my fiancé Ken and I decided to take a trip to Canada. First, we went to see Niagara Falls. After that, we drove to Toronto for a couple of days since the city was not too far from where we were. We wanted to visit the museums there, do some shopping, and dine out in a couple of the nicer restaurants. Toronto was so nice, and especially clean. We were both impressed with the city.

After we arrived at the hotel and had checked in, we parked in the parking garage. Then we grabbed our luggage and got out of the car. We headed for the garage elevator, so tired and anxious to get up to our room. When the elevator door in the parking garage opened up for us, Ken got on it with our luggage. I was right behind him. All of a sudden I remembered I had left my cell phone in the car. I quickly panicked and jumped off the elevator as the door started closing. Immediately, I heard Ken yell for me to get back on, but it was too late. The door had already closed shut. Ken had sounded so frustrated with me, but I couldn't help the way I felt. I could not take the elevator without my cell phone. I was too afraid and insecure.

I just stood there in the parking lot not knowing what to do. Ken had the keys to the car so I had no place to go. I was hoping he would come back down for me, or else I would be spending the night in the hotel garage parking lot. I knew if I weren't capable of getting on the elevator with Ken, I sure couldn't get back on it without him. Ken knew how I felt, so I was certain he would come back for me. I waited by the car patiently for his return.

About two minutes later, I found out how much Ken loved me. He had come back for me, but he was not a happy camper. I could tell he was upset as he walked back to the car to get my cell phone. He grabbed the phone, slammed the car door shut, and mumbled a few distasteful words under his breath. I was sure he was just tired and taking his frustration out on me.

The two of us got back on the elevator and headed for our room. Of course, Ken lectured me the entire way up about how much time I had cost us. He told me that my claustrophobic behavior was getting very old to him, and he was losing patience with me. He said he could not understand my fear, and I needed to get over it in a hurry. He also said he was not going to go out of his way again to pacify my baby habits. I felt as though I had been slapped in the face by him instead of feeling loved by him. His cruel words had hurt me a lot, but what could I do? *I know he's probably right, but I can't help the way I feel,* I thought. *Oh well. Tomorrow will hopefully be a new and better day*, I assured myself.

The next morning as the two of us were walking down the street, Ken spotted a very tall building. He told me that he had heard there was a restaurant located on the top floor. We both stared high in the air, looking at the monster building. It looked as though it were the tallest one in the entire city. Ken laughed out loud, and then asked me if I'd like to have dinner there that night. I laughed back, and said, "Yes, as a matter of fact, I would love to have dinner there." I asked Ken if he were buying, and he said, "Yes, if you are brave enough to get on that elevator and go all the way to the top. I'll buy." I laughed and said, "As long as I have my cell phone with me, I'll go anywhere." Ken said, "Dory, I'm going to hold you to those words."

Of course I was afraid just thinking about going all the way to the top of that building. I remember wishing several times that day that I would not have made the dinner deal with Ken, but I had. *I will have to follow through with it now,* I thought. *Maybe this will be good for me. Maybe if I face my biggest fear, I will get over it, and become stronger and braver. Nevertheless, I feel a sick feeling in the pit of my belly, but I know I have to go up and have dinner with my guy. Besides, I have my cell phone as my security blanket. I can do this,* I kept telling myself over and over.

The afternoon was quickly drawing to an end. What I had been secretly doing all day was constantly thinking up silly excuses in my mind to get out of going to dinner that night. I did not have the guts to break them out to Ken, though. I knew he wouldn't believe me anyway. I made up my mind I had to go, just as I had told him I would, as much as I was dreading it.

Around seven o'clock that night Ken and I stood in line to get on the elevator, and when it was our turn, we were the first two people to be led on. I stood there carefully watching, and it seemed to me that there were too many people going up at the same time. *Gee! It's getting so crowded!* I thought. I quickly spoke up, and said, "I think we have enough people on this elevator now." I did not know there was a lady attendant working the elevator who would be taking us up to the top floor. The lady worker looked around and smiled at me, and she was quick to tell me that she was keeping a head count, and would let me know when there were enough people on the elevator. I told her I was sorry, trying to smile back at her.

Wow! I feel so silly, and I'm wishing I could be anywhere but where I am. Ken was right. I'm wanting with all my heart to back out of going up, but it's a little late now, I thought. *The door is slowly closing.*

Standing on the elevator next to me was a group of ten guys. They were all laughing and joking around, telling me to close my eyes and relax. I did as they said. I only opened my eyes for a moment and all I saw were the different buildings flashing briefly through the glass elevator window as we went up. It was the longest elevator ride I had ever taken. I quickly closed my eyes shut again until we stopped and the elevator door safely opened. Everyone let me get off first, knowing I was frightened. I breathed a deep sigh of relief as the waiter led us to our table inside the restaurant.

I sat down in the chair, and then looked up at Ken. He was sitting directly across from me. *Oh my!* I thought to myself. Ken's face was as white as a ghost, and his lips were even whiter. He was so pale. I asked him if he were okay, and he said, "No, Dory, I'm not." I immediately called the waiter over to our table, and told him I was worried about my boyfriend because of the way he looked and what he had said. I wondered if Ken were having a heart attack. I became very concerned for him. The waiter asked Ken if he were afraid of heights. Ken said, "No, I don't think so." He talked to Ken for a couple more minutes, and then said, "Sir, I really do think you have a fear of heights, and a cold beer will probably make you feel better." Of course, Ken smiled and told him to bring him one. *Wow! I'm so shocked that Ken is showing worry of anything. He has never displayed one single sign of this sort of behavior since I have known him, so why now?* I wondered. I couldn't help but grab my camera to take Ken's picture. *I never want him to forget his fear of heights. Maybe he will go a little easier on me in the future about my elevator apprehension,* I thought. Ken was finally starting to get his color back, so I was sure he'd be okay. I drank a beer with him as we laughed about the picture I took that would hopefully show his white face and lips. "For once the tables have turned," I told Ken as I laughed out loud. Ken laughed again, too.

Amazed by the scenery, I got up from the chair and walked around as the entire room slowly turned showing off the city's gigantic buildings. When Ken saw me leaning over by one of the big windows, he yelled for me to come back to the table and sit down. He asked me if I were crazy or had lost my mind, because he could not believe I was getting so close to the windows. "We are too far up for you to be doing that," Ken said. I just laughed at him while saying, "I'm not terrified of heights Ken, only elevators and closed-in places." Ken told me how well he remembered, and he also told me he was so sorry for the things he had said to me in the past about my fear and anxiety. He went on to say that he would never give me a hard time again concerning this. Of course, I thanked him for that, and I was sure he meant it.

After the two of us finished eating and had taken the elevator back down to the first floor, Ken told me that the waiter told him about a shop located directly below the restaurant. The waiter said the room had a glass floor and that we could have walked on it while seeing everything below us. Ken told me he did not want to tell me about it until we had gotten back down to the ground floor, for fear I might want to visit the store with the glass floor. I just laughed and told him he was probably right.

The next day as we were leaving the hotel, I noticed a man selling white tee shirts. When I picked one up to look at it, I saw a picture of the restaurant we had visited printed on the front of it. I could not resist buying one for Ken to take home with him as a souvenir gift. I wanted him to always have the shirt to remind him of his fear of heights. Needless to say, I never want him to forget about it. To this day, and out of love, I still do not mind telling my friend that **"what goes around comes around."**

Dawg

Be proud of your name; since birth it became
Something you need and something that's free.

D.J. DeSai

Some are born with a name they love, and some are not. Some grow to love their names with time, and some never do. There are a few folks who have changed their names for one reason or another, and some who have no choice but to keep them until death do them part. However, we have no control over the name we are given at birth, because it is not our decision. I wonder how much happier we would be if we could choose our own names. I also often wonder if, like people, pets like or dislike their names.

My boyfriend, Chevy, came over one day with an Easter basket in his hand. He handed me the basket and inside it was a gift that would soon become my bundle of joy. Chevy had bought me the cutest little apricot toy poodle. The puppy was so tiny that I could hold him in the palm of my hand. It didn't take me very long to name my pet, because everyone who came in contact with him called him Baby. It also didn't take long for everyone to fall in love with my little puppy named Baby.

During this time my dad was very ill, and a few weeks after Chevy gave me the poodle, my dad passed away. I'm not sure I would have survived the loss of my dear dad if I had not been given the sweet puppy to console me and to help me through the mourning process. I became very attached to Baby, and also he to me. Although Baby required a lot of attention, he was just what I needed at that time.

A few months later, Chevy started showing a few signs of jealousy concerning my poodle. His behavior surprised me, because he was the one who had given me the puppy. He kept telling me that he would love to have a dog for himself. Chevy drove a semi-truck for a living, and oftentimes he would become very lonely while traveling from state to state. He told me he wanted a dog that he could take on the road with him. "Yes!" I told Chevy. "I think you need a dog, too." He said, "Dory, I agree. I do want one."

A few days later, I decided I would buy Chevy a puppy. I was so grateful for the poodle he had bought for me. Yes, I would return the sweet favor, and I couldn't wait to surprise him with it. I searched and searched for the right puppy for him, and finally I found a Border collie. I knew Chevy wanted a larger dog than my poodle, so I felt sure he would appreciate a full-blooded intelligent dog like the collie. I couldn't wait to see him so I could give him the gift I had chosen for him.

Oh! I did surprise Chevy alright. At first, he spent all of his time with the dog. But then he took him on only two road trips with him. Afterwards, he told me it just wasn't working out like he had thought it would and he didn't think it was a good idea for him to take the collie on the road with him again. He said the puppy was too high strung; therefore, the dog would not sit in the truck for that many hours at a time. He told me that he was finding it difficult to drive his truck and entertain his pet at the same time.

I understood what Chevy was saying to me, but it was a little late for him to be finding this out now. "I can't believe it!" I told Chevy. "Maybe I should have given you a dog that you could take with you on a trial run first!" I was upset! I had already bought the puppy, and I was sure I could not return him to the owner. *What in the world will I do now?* I wondered. I assured Chevy that the only problem was that the puppy was still young and vibrant. I told him that, in due time, the dog would settle down tremendously. Chevy told me he could not take that chance, and he hoped I understood. He said he could not afford to wreck his truck because of a dog. He had made his mind up, and that was the end of our conversation.

While trying to understand Chevy's concerns, I knew who would be stuck taking care of the collie. I couldn't help being upset with his decision because, honestly, I had never asked for one dog, and now I had two. Don't get me wrong. I loved the poodle that Chevy had given me, but he was a handful. Needless to say, I did not have as much free time as I liked and was accustomed to. It took a lot to care for a dog. It was also very costly to own one, too. I had the expenses of the dog's shots and his grooming. I also had the kennel bills to pay when I wanted to go out of town on a vacation. After some serious thinking, I decided I would keep the collie myself for a few weeks because I was sure Chevy would change his mind about taking him out on the road with him again. He just needed a little time for the puppy to settle down.

A few more weeks went by when I asked Chevy to take the collie with him again. He was still very firm, telling me no. He said, "Truck driving is too dangerous and I cannot risk it." He said he did not think the dog would ever relax enough to be content just riding down the road with him. He thought it would be unfair to the collie, and he admitted he had made a huge mistake by thinking it would work out. He told me he was sorry again for thinking he wanted a dog.

"Oh my God!" I prayed out loud. "What will I do with another dog?" I asked the Lord to help me to deal with the pet situation. This had not worked out the way I had planned. I had the feeling I knew where this entire dilemma was going and yes, I was right. Guess who would soon become the proud owner of two dogs? Yes, it would be me. I knew I may as well get used to it, because my two children and I had already become attached to the collie. There would be no giving him back now.

A couple more weeks went by and no one had come up with a name for the puppy. I tried to name him myself, but every time I'd come up with something I liked, Chevy or one of my children would find something wrong with it. The three of them would tell me it wasn't fair. They said it was their turn to name the new dog since I was the one who had named the poodle, Baby. Looking back on the situation now, I realize I should have taken complete control of the dog naming. I should have told all three of them that since I was the one who was taking care of the collie, I would be the one naming him, too, end of story.

However, I decided to give in to all their ideas, and allow one of them to come up with a unique name for the puppy. I liked the name Homer, but no one else did. I continued to wait patiently, hoping everyone would agree on something very soon. The collie desperately needed a name.

Meanwhile, I started calling the dog "Dawg," because unfortunately, he was still nameless. The thought crossed my mind that he may never be blessed with a name. After a couple more weeks went by, the collie started answering to the name "Dawg." It was really quite humorous, because the name had rubbed off on all of us by then. Soon, everyone was calling the collie "Dawg." It was also during the same time period when most of the teenagers were calling each other "dog," so the name "Dawg" just seemed to fit right in with the trend.

Even though I am quite sure I could have come up with a name much more original than "Dawg," I feel this was the name that was meant to be for him all along. My Border collie has also turned out to be the smartest dog I have ever owned. He can even sing! Well, he can howl, and make it sound as though he's singing. Now, I wouldn't take a million dollars for my loving, beautiful, and intelligent dog named **"Dawg."**

Winning Money

When you hear a blessing knock at your door,
Expect much more than you had before.

D.J. DeSai

I have often heard it said that certain things can happen in sets of threes around the same time period. I believe this. For instance, once my friend's dog died; one week later my relative's dog passed on, and a few days later my own dog died. These three related incidents were not good things, but other times things that happen coincidently can be an awesome blessing. Here is a sweet example of that.

It was a beautiful, sunny, seventy degree Derby Day in Louisville, Kentucky, and many people were getting ready to watch the most amazing horse race of the year. I could feel a very special kind of magic in the air, so the last place I really wanted to be was at work, but I had to be. It was a Saturday, which was the busiest day of the week. Thank God, my boss had always closed the business early on Derby Day. I couldn't wait to get out of there into the beautiful, sunshiny day with everyone else in the city.

The horses were getting ready to run for the roses later that afternoon, and the town was not only filled up with its own residential people, but also with people traveling from different places all over the world. Everyone was waiting in anticipation to see which horse would end up in the winner's circle. I couldn't wait either. I was more than excited! I was Derby crazed!

Earlier that afternoon I decided to make up a Derby jackpot at my workplace, just as I had every year. Most everyone always looked forward to drawing a horse out, so they would have a special one to pull for. A huge amount of the Louisville natives did not care anything about going to the Derby, because of the large crowd. Also, there were so many horses in the race that it was almost impossible to guess the winner, so picking one out of a jackpot was easy enough. Besides, everyone had the same odds of winning by doing it this way.

I let some of the clients and co-workers draw a ticket out first. I wanted to make sure that everyone who wanted one got one. Then I asked a co-worker to hold the jar while I drew mine out. When I looked at my ticket, I was so happy. The horse I had drawn was named "Winning Colors." This horse was the only filly in the Derby race. I was so proud to have drawn this one out, because I liked the horse a lot. I had hoped the filly would beat all the other horses by a landslide. I smiled to myself as I put the ticket safely inside my purse. There were a few other horse picks left in the jar for some of the other clients who would probably come in later that day. No doubt, they would all get sold before the work day was over.

A few minutes later the shop phone rang. It was my turn to answer it, and I was glad I had. It was my girlfriend Sandy reminding me of the Derby party she was having that afternoon. The party would probably run into the wee hours of the night, too, she said. I told Sandy yes, that I was planning to come to her party but I didn't know what time I would get there. I went on to tell her that I had a few things to do after work, while assuring my friend that I would arrive long before the party was over. Sandy reminded me that she had lots of good food, drink, music, and fun things to participate in at her party. I smiled with delight as I thanked Sandy for the invitation. I reminded her again that I would definitely be there, and we hung the phones up.

A couple of hours later I walked over to the mini market next to my workplace to pick up a soda. When I laid my drink down on the counter to pay for it, Herb the store manager held out a big red plastic glass in front of me. It was another Derby jackpot. Herb asked me if I wanted to draw one out. I smiled at him as I shook my head, no. I told him I had already drawn one out of our own jackpot at work, and I liked the horse I had drawn. I thanked him for the offer, though, while telling him I did not want to draw again, because I could not draw a better horse than the one I already had. Herb laughed as he told me he thought I needed to draw one more time. He told me there was only one ticket left in the glass, and he wanted to get rid of it so he could go on home. I thought about it another few seconds before telling him to give it to me. I told Herb I guessed I could spare another dollar bill on Derby Day. He chuckled out loud as he explained to me that his jackpot was a five-dollar jackpot instead of a one-dollar one. Immediately, I shook my head no again, telling him thanks but no thanks. I told him his jackpot was a little too rich for my blood so I'd have to pass. Herb said, "Come on, Dory. Don't be so cheap," as he laughed out loud again and told me I needed to go ahead and draw the last horse out. I was getting tired of his begging and pleading with me, so I finally decided to give in to him. I really needed to get back to work.

Half-heartedly, I pulled a five-dollar bill out of my wallet and gave it to Herb while still thinking it was probably too much to spend on a jackpot. *Oh well! It is Derby Day,* I thought to myself. I didn't really want to draw again, but I told myself this certain day only comes around once a year, so I tried to justify it.

I pulled the last tiny piece of paper out of the jackpot, and quickly opened it up before leaving the store. "Oh my goodness!" I screamed out to Herb. "I love this horse!" I couldn't believe my eyes. I had drawn the same one that I had drawn from the one-dollar jackpot at my workplace. "Yes, I drew Winning Colors again!" I shouted. Needless to say, no one in the whole wide world could have told me that the filly wasn't going to win the Kentucky Derby race that day. I walked out of the store feeling very confident about both jackpots. I was so happy, and seriously thinking about making a bet on my favorite horse. After all, I had drawn it twice. *The odds of this happening must be astronomical,* I thought to myself. "Yippee!" I shouted.

The work day went by quickly, and it was soon time for me to head home. I had sold all of the Derby tickets in the jackpot, so I carefully counted the money, making sure it was all there before putting it in a sealed envelope. I decided to leave it at the shop for the Derby winner to pick up the following week. I quickly stored it safely inside a drawer before leaving.

After arriving home, I was certain I needed to take a nap before going to Sandy's party. I didn't really want to lose any part of the day, but I was feeling tired. As I was just getting ready to sit down and relax, I heard the phone ring. It was Sandy telling me to hurry up and get to her party, because the Derby race would soon be running. I told her that I would try to make it before the race, but I couldn't promise. I went on to explain to her that I was feeling a bit tired.

Before we said our goodbyes, Sandy told me she was going to go ahead and draw a horse pick for me from her jackpot since she was afraid I wouldn't get to draw one if I got there too late. "Besides, Dory, there is only one ticket left", Sandy told me. I was quick to tell her not to draw one out for me. I told her I had already drawn out of two other jackpots earlier, and that was more than enough. Sandy told me she would not take no for an answer. She said she wanted me to have the last horse pick in her jackpot. "I'll put a dollar in for you Dory, and you can pay me back if you win." I continued to tell Sandy no, but needless to say, she would not hear of it. She said she was drawing the ticket as we were speaking, and for me not to hang the phone up until she told me what horse she'd drawn for me.

A few seconds later, I heard Sandy mumble, "You've got Winning Colors." "Wow!" I said with disbelief in my voice. I was flabbergasted! I thanked Sandy and told her I would see her soon as we hung up the phones. I had decided I would tell her about my one-horse draws in three jackpots later when there was more time. *For now, I need to rest, but I can't help but wonder, though, how in the world one person can draw from three jackpots in one day and draw the same horse out every time. It almost seems absurd*, I thought to myself.

After thinking about the Derby race for a few more minutes, I decided to call another friend to see if I could place a bet on my choice horse, Winning Colors. Yes, I had claimed the filly in my heart by then. I felt as though there was nothing else left to do but to bet on the horse. The filly was haunting my heart. *Besides, it's Derby Day*, I told myself, *and I have drawn the horse three times. I have to bet on her or I will feel bad if I don't.*

My friend answered the phone and told me yes, there was still time to make a bet. I told him I wanted ten dollars across the board which meant ten dollars to win, ten dollars to place, and ten dollars to show. This would cost me a total of thirty dollars. I had never made it a habit of betting that much money on one race, but I had a big feeling about the filly. It must have been my "one-horse out of three jackpots" logic. My friend told me that my bet was on, so I hung the phone up, wondering if I were crazy or on some kind of lucky streak. I guessed I would find out soon enough, though, because the horses would soon be running.

I poured myself a glass of red wine. Then I lay down on the sofa to relax for a minute. I was starting to feel some anxiety, so I knew I needed to rest before going to Sandy's party. I looked up at my television screen and saw the Derby race would be running in exactly one hour. I closed my eyes and fell asleep for about forty-five minutes. When I awakened, I felt refreshed. The nap was exactly what I needed.

I got up from the sofa, quickly showered, and got dressed. I was putting on my make-up when I glanced over and saw the horses lining up in the gate. "It's Derby time!" I yelled. The horses were getting ready to run for the roses. I also thought I saw the filly, Winning Colors, throw her head back, as if to say she was confident this race would belong to her. With a grin on my face, I started reminiscing about my day all over again in my head. *Gee! I still cannot believe I drew the filly out of three jackpots. I just know I'm going to win the big Derby race,* I thought to myself.

Suddenly, I heard the track announcer say, "And they're off." The gate flew open and I watched the horses quickly take off down the stretch. I couldn't tell which one had taken the lead. I did not even know the number of the filly, but I would soon find out which one would win. They were moving so fast, because they were all on the same mission. They were all racing to win as they fled down the track like lightning past the last turn for home. As the horses were getting closer to the finish line, I saw the number six horse take the lead. The number six horse also made it to the finish line first. I was so excited that I didn't really care who had won the race. I dearly loved Derby time. I also loved watching the horses run.

"Oh my God!" I shouted out to heaven. I could not believe my ears, as I heard the announcer say, "The winner of the Kentucky Derby race is the filly, Winning Colors." *What a blessing from above!* I thought to myself. I could feel my heart beating faster and faster as I started jumping up and down. I was filled with joy! I was so happy that my horse had crossed the finish line first. *I won! Yes! I won three times. No! I won more than three times, because I bet on the filly to win, place, and show,* I thought to myself. I started adding my money that I had won in my head as I continued to make my last preparations to get ready to leave to go to Sandy's party. "I love Winning Colors!" I shouted. I was dancing on cloud nine. This was my Derby Day. I thanked the Lord again.

I started out the front door as my phone rang. It was Sandy telling me that I had won the jackpot. She was so happy for me, and she had to have known that I was thrilled too, by the sound of my voice. I made up my mind to surprise Sandy with half of my jackpot winnings, since she was the one who had drawn the lucky horse from the pot. I told her I was on my way to her party, and we hung the phones up.

That night I shared my winnings with Sandy, while we both celebrated the Derby with the rest of our friends at the party. We all had a great time talking, singing, laughing, and just hanging out together. Everyone congratulated me on my winnings, and they were all very glad for me. Yes, friends were great, but I couldn't take my mind off the filly that had won the Derby race. I felt so lucky, but more than that, I felt so blessed.

What a fabulous Derby race in Louisville, Kentucky! Yes, it was a profitable, blissful and most delightful day for me, and I was so very grateful for it. It wasn't just the money that had filled my heart with pleasure. It was the way it had all fallen into place. Someone told me that lady luck had taken me under her wings for the entire day, but I chose to give all the glory to my Lord Jesus Christ. Even though the jockey led that beautiful filly, Winning Colors, to victory lane, I thanked God for the money. Yes, it was a Derby Day that was filled with more than Winning Colors. For me, it was filled with **"winning money."**

Saved Again

Better not to be sorry, instead be safe,
If you have a gut feeling, don't count it as waste.

D.J. DeSai

During my past, I have found myself in situations a few times where I should have probably made verbal suggestions concerning someone else's well being, but I didn't. Occasionally, though, I've found out later that by keeping quiet about a certain problem was probably for the best. Thank God, I made the right decision during this trial, because there was so much at stake. If I had chosen to just let it go, I am sure this person would have lost his life.

A friend of mine named Phillip started complaining to me one day about not feeling well. I had stopped by his house to see if he wanted to go to a movie with me. While I was there, Phillip told me that he had already missed a couple days of work. He went on to explain to me that his symptoms consisted of feeling tired and run down while experiencing an aching all over his entire body. It sounded like the flu virus to me so I suggested that he take something to help him rest that night. I asked him if he had a fever, but he said he didn't think so. I told him he needed to check his temperature and if he continued to feel worse, he should contact his family physician. Phillip thanked me for my concern, and told me he would do it, as I left his home.

The next morning, I decided to give Phillip a call to see how he was doing. After letting the phone ring several times, I hung it up, assuming he was feeling better and had gone back to work. Later that afternoon, I called his office. His co-worker told me that Phillip had not shown up for work yet, and that he had not called to inform anyone that he wasn't coming in. She went on to say that this was so un-like him. She seemed extremely concerned about him, too. I felt in my own heart that something must be very wrong, so I had to find out for myself. I decided I would take a break from my workplace and go check on him.

After I hung the phone up, I drove to Phillip's home and knocked on his door. There was no answer, although his car was sitting in the driveway in the same place as it had been the day before when I had visited him. I continued to knock on the door, while calling Phillip's phone number over and over. Still, there was no answer from him, and I started getting more worried by the minute.

Thank God Phillip finally answered the door. He appeared very pale and distraught to me. As long as I had known him, I had never seen him look as bad as he did at that very moment. I asked him if he were getting any better, feeling sure he couldn't be by the way he looked. He acted as though he were in a distant trance. He just stood there staring at me with his eyes half closed. I started wondering if he even recognized me or anything else for that matter. I reached out and touched his forehead with my hand. Gee wiz! He was scalding hot! I told Phillip he was burning up with fever, and asked him if he had taken anything for it. I reminded him that we had talked about this the night before.

Finally he spoke, telling me that he had not taken any medicine yet. He assured me, though, that he was going to take something, as he started slowly closing the door in my face. He told me that he was so tired, and needed to go back to bed. Before I could say another word, Phillip had shut the door. I tried to open it back up, but it was locked. I just stood there stunned from worry about my friend's health condition, wondering what I should do about it. I was sure I needed to do something but I wasn't sure what my boundaries were when it came to him. He acted as though he did not want me there, but I wondered if he was too sick to know what he needed. I had to find out.

When I got back into my car and looked at my watch, I knew I should get back to work. I pulled out of Phillip's driveway and headed down the road. Then I called my boss to tell him that I was on my way back, and would be there shortly. While I was driving, Phillip's face kept haunting my mind, so I was having a real hard time feeling okay about leaving him. *What if Phillip is too sick to take care of himself? What if he needs immediate medical attention? Will I ever forgive myself if something terrible happens to him?* These questions kept playing in my mind. I was very worried.

I knew I couldn't go back to work feeling this way. Quickly, I turned my car back around and headed back to Phillip's house. I called my shop again to tell my boss that I would not be coming back because I needed to take care of a friend. After I explained what was going on, my boss agreed, telling me not to worry about anything at work. He told me to keep him informed as to what was going on. I thanked him and hung the phone up, driving as fast as I could to get back to Phillip's home.

When I pulled back into the driveway, I tooted my horn two or three times, hoping to get Phillip's attention before knocking aggressively on his door again. It didn't work. I rushed out of the car, ran to the front porch, and started frantically ringing his doorbell. I wanted to let him know that I meant business this time. I was not going to leave him for a second time until I knew for sure that he was okay.

It took a few minutes, but thank God Phillip opened the door again as sluggishly as he had before. He still had that same colorless look on his face. I knew he must be wondering why I had returned so suddenly, but I didn't give him the time to even ask why. I grabbed hold of the door immediately, opening it up all the way. Then I let myself in the house. I told Phillip that I had come back to take him to the doctor. He argued with me at first but then he said okay. I told him to go get ready, and I would wait for him in my car. He thanked me.

A couple minutes later, Phillip walked out the front door and got in the car. I couldn't help but grin when I saw what he was wearing. He still had on his housecoat as he sat down in the passenger's seat. The poor guy was nearly out of it, although I was sure it was because of his high fever. Knowing that he was practically unaware, and feeling so rotten, I hated telling him he had to go back into the house and change his clothes. I tried to make a joke out of it saying, "Phillip, you need to lose the housecoat, and put on a shirt and a pair of jeans." By this time, though, I was sure I was making the right decision by taking him to the doctor. He was definitely not thinking straight and surely needed someone's help.

While sitting in my car waiting, I wondered if I might need to go back into the house and chase Phillip back out. I would have done just that too, if I had needed to. This time I was taking full responsibility for his actions and his sickness. In my eyes, there was nothing he could do nor say about it anymore. He needed to see a doctor, and I would see to it that he did.

When we arrived at the doctor's office, I walked in with Phillip. I asked him if he wanted me to go with him when they called him back to see the doctor. He said, yes. He wanted my company. I felt good about being there for my friend. I knew how bad he must be feeling, because he had not even mentioned smoking a cigarette since I had been with him. Phillip was a chain smoker. He lived to smoke.

Soon, the nurse called him to the back room to test his vital signs. She weighed him, took his temperature, his blood pressure, and listened to his heart beat. I wasn't surprised when the nurse said that Phillip's temperature was 103.5 degrees. I knew it had to be high, because his skin felt so hot. A few minutes later, the nurse took him to another room for x-rays. I waited. Ten minutes later, they returned.

Shortly afterwards, the doctor came in with Phillip's chart. He had a very puzzled look on his face while telling the two of us that it was very imperative for Phillip to be admitted to a hospital immediately. The doctor said that he was very sick, dehydrated, and needed to be treated without delay. He said that he had pneumonia. The doctor walked closer to us while showing us the x-rays and what was on them. He said that Phillip had several spots on his lungs, being the first signs of emphysema. He also said he was a very sick man, and it would have been deadly if one more day had gone by without treatment. He felt sure that Phillip may not have made it one more night. "Without treatment, the fever and dehydration would have killed him much sooner than later," the doctor said.

"Oh my God," I whispered to the Lord. *What if I hadn't turned my car around and went back to pick him up? Could I have forgiven myself if he had passed away?* I wondered. I was in a complete daze, standing there thinking of only negative but realistic thoughts. I hardly remember saying yes when the doctor asked me if I could drive Phillip to the nearest hospital for admission. He told me it was very important for us to go at once. I told the doctor I would do it, as Phillip and I left the office in a hurry.

After rushing out the door and getting in the car, Phillip just sat there staring into space. I was quite sure I knew what he was thinking. The doctor had really gotten on him about his smoking cigarettes. He told him that he would not live much longer if he did not quit. Phillip had told the doctor he wanted to quit and I had actually believed him, although I was certain it would be one of the hardest things he would ever do in his life. It was a fact that he loved his cigarettes, probably as much as life itself. I was happy to hear him tell the doctor that he would quit, though, because I knew his health would be in great danger if he didn't. I was concerned about the spots on his lungs, too, but I did not say too much to him about it. I was sure it had to be weighing on his mind enough already. I decided it was best not to add insult to injury. He was feeling so awful, having all the symptoms of pneumonia.

As we walked into the emergency room door of the hospital, I noticed Phillip was moving very slowly. I was sure he was running out of energy because he was so dehydrated, sick, and weak. We made it to the admission center, and I could not believe all the paperwork that was involved when someone was so sick and needing immediate medical attention. It seemed as though it took hours to fill out all the papers. *Poor Phillip,* I kept thinking.

Finally, we were told to go sit in the emergency room waiting area. The receptionist said it shouldn't take long for Phillip to be called, and then he would be admitted to his room. Wrong! After two to three hours of just sitting and waiting, I went up to the information center and asked the same lady how much longer it would be. She told me she did not know, because there were still people ahead of us to be admitted. She told me that we would just have to wait, as everyone else had to. I wondered if she knew how sick Phillip really was. I also wondered if she even cared. I tried not to throw blame at anyone, but it wasn't easy.

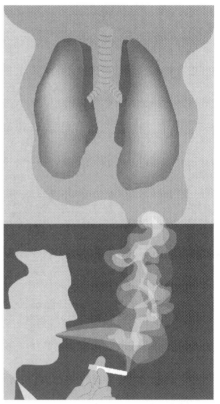

Another hour went by before Phillip's name was finally called. He was looking so much punier by then, and had almost passed out in the waiting room chair. Thank God, the nurse brought down a wheelchair for him. Then she took him to the elevator and on up to the fifth floor.

When we got to the room, the nurse helped Phillip out of the chair. Then he sat down on the bed. He still had his clothes on. Wow! He looked so unhealthy. My heart went out to him. I was so concerned. It didn't take him too long to lie all the way down on the bed. I only hoped it wouldn't be long before they would give him something to help him rest and bring his fever down. His skin was so hot and clammy, although he was shivering as if he were freezing cold. I put a pillow under his head, and covered his body with a blanket as he lay there on the hospital bed still dressed and waiting for assistance.

After several more minutes, I wondered if Phillip would get any attention or if he would just lie there and die while waiting. I was getting very frustrated. I watched as the clock slowly moved and, still, no one had come into the room. I walked to the nurse's station to try and find out what was going on, but no one had time to stop and talk to me. Everyone seemed to be in a big hurry. I walked back into Phillip's room feeling helpless. I also felt as though I was in the way of all the hospital workers as they kept rushing by me. I wanted so badly to do something positive for my good friend Phillip, who was still lying there on the bed. He had to be feeling miserable, and all the while I stood there looking at him, the angrier I became. *Oh my goodness!* I thought to myself. *How much longer will Phillip have to lie on the hospital bed with all his clothes on? He has such a high fever and needs medical attention at once.* I was almost ready to pick a fight. Yes, I was starting to feel a little redneck by then.

I walked back out into the hallway but this time I made up my mind I was not going to move until someone paid attention to me. I stepped right in front of one of the nurses and explained to her that my friend was burning up with fever. I told her that he was lying on the bed with his clothes on, and needed urgent care. I also told her that it had taken the emergency room clerks several hours to admit him to his room. Now, it had been almost two more hours, and no one had even come in to check on him or to offer him care. I asked her what kind of hospital would just let someone lay there and suffer like that. I told the nurse that I had taken Phillip to the doctor that morning because I was worried that he may not make it, and the doctor had confirmed that he was a very sick man just a few hours prior. I went on to tell the nurse that I was more worried about him now, even though he had finally been checked in to the hospital.

Thank God, the nurse instantly came into Phillip's room and helped him change into a hospital gown. Then she proceeded to give him fluids intravenously. Someone had finally taken an interest. The nurse was very apologetic, and I was so thankful for her concern. I felt a little guilty about jumping on to her, but I had to do what I had to do for Phillip's sake. I was sure he would have done the same for me.

After Phillip was given full-time care, I knew he needed to rest. I whispered in his ear to tell him I was leaving for a few minutes to go pick up some things he would need while staying in the hospital. I told him I would take his house key with me, stop by his place, and then come right back. Phillip shook his head yes, and then closed his eyes again.

I quietly exited Phillip's room, and then left the hospital. I called my workplace and told my co-workers what was going on. They were very understanding, and told me to take all the time I needed. I thanked them, and then hung up the phone. Then I drove to Phillip's house to get the necessities he needed for his hospital stay.

For the next several days, I continued to visit Phillip at the hospital, and he was very thankful each time. He said, "Dory, you saved my life by taking off from work, and taking me to the doctor and the hospital." I told him that he would have done the same for me if I would have needed him to. He agreed.

Phillip was in the hospital for a week, and then the doctor sent him home. He gave Phillip a prescription to help him quit smoking cigarettes. I did not see him smoke for the next couple of months, and I continued to tell him how proud I was of him. Quitting smoking was a very big accomplishment, and I told him so.

A few weeks later, I stopped by Phillip's home one day unexpectedly. I did not think of calling him first, but I was sure it didn't matter. We were very close friends. When I got there, he was sitting on the front porch. It didn't take long for me to notice that he was smoking a cigarette. The moment Phillip saw me, he immediately tried to put it out, but he wasn't fast enough. Then he started making excuses to me for his smoking. I told him it was not really any of my business, but I asked him why he had started again after taking the medicine to stop. He told me that the past few days he had felt better than he had in a very long time, so he didn't see the harm in smoking a little. I reminded him of the spots on his lungs, and what the doctor had told him about his emphysema. Phillip just dropped his head without saying anything else. Evidently, the cigarettes seemed more important to Phillip than his lungs were, so I decided to shut up about it. Phillip would quit when he was ready to.

It has been five years now since Phillip's hospital stay, and he is still smoking cigarettes. He's smoking just as many now, if not more than he was then. I still don't say anything about it, because I hate the thought of him thinking I'm preaching to him. I'm so concerned about him, though, because I care so much for him as my friend. I keep remembering the old saying, "You can lead a horse to water, but you can't make him drink."

What else can I do? I wondered. I have decided to pray for my friend, and leave his health care in the Lord's hands.

Phillip still tells me that I saved his life that day, but I wonder if that is really true. I have always believed that a person cannot die unless Jesus says it is time. This thought still gives me hope that if my friend Phillip was saved once by my good deed, then by the grace of God and his faith in Jesus Christ, I believe he most certainly can be **"saved again."**

Sick For a Fish

I'd love to try many things in my life,
But I may not try twice if once wasn't all right.

D.J. DeSai

Has there ever been something in your life that you have always wanted to experience and then finally the day came and you got the chance to do it? Did you fantasize about that certain event for so long that when you did get to do it, you were somewhat let down? I can certainly relate to that feeling in this story.

I've often imagined what it might feel like to catch a fish, and I have had very high hopes that I would get to do this sometime during my life. The two times I had gone fishing, I had no luck with the pole. The first time I went, I did not catch anything. The second time, I hooked one but it accidentally got away from me. On second thought, the real reason the fish probably got away was because of my lack of knowledge. Nevertheless, I told myself that someday I would take the time to go fishing again, and hopefully learn how to. I was brought up in the country so I surely didn't want to leave this world not knowing what it felt like to catch one.

One day while I was vacationing in Florida with family and friends, a girlfriend named Cindy asked me to go deep sea fishing with her. I told Cindy yes, that I definitely wanted to go. Feeling excited, I kept thinking about how I had always wanted to catch a fish and never had. I couldn't wait to get out in the deep blue ocean and try my hand at it once again. *Surely, I will have better luck this time,* I thought.

The morning Cindy and I decided to go, I got up early so I could eat and drink a little something before we took off. I knew it would be a long day at sea, and I did not want to take a chance of getting dehydrated in the hot sun. Around ten o'clock I met my friend at the dock, and we stood in line for our turn to go out on the boat. Two men who worked there were in charge of taking the two of us deep sea fishing. I wondered why several of the employees were standing there chatting with each other for so long while we waited. "Oh well. I've waited this long to catch a fish; I can wait a little longer," I told Cindy. We found out later that the employees were talking about the water being so rough, and they wondered if they should cancel all the deep sea fishing trips that morning because of it.

Finally, the workers got the okay from the office manager to go ahead and go, so Cindy and I climbed on board with them, and we took off. The ocean wind and water was blowing so hard in my face, and it felt wonderful. I remember thinking I would love to have their job, because it would probably be so much fun that it wouldn't even seem like work. I yelled out, "I think you all 'have it made in the shade' by getting to take people out on the boat to fish every day and getting paid for it, too." One man just smiled and said, "Yes, Dory, but some days the water gets very rough." He pointed out at the super high waves and told me that sometimes it gets even worse than that. I told him it did not seem rough to me, but I was not the one driving the boat, so what did I know? He just laughed at my comments, and I laughed back.

Homer, the driver, drove the boat a few miles out to sea before coming to a halt. I asked him why we were stopping and he said it was time to fish. I was so happy because I just knew this was my day to catch my first big one. There was excitement in the air and in the water. Excitement was definitely in my stomach, too. The more I looked out at the climbing waves and the moving water, the dizzier I became. There was also a gassy smell coming out of the engine and this was not helping me feel any better either.

Feeling sicker than I had felt in a very long time, I told Homer that I needed to sit down. "Oh my!" I whispered to myself. I was not feeling well at all. Homer told me he thought that my sitting was a good idea, but immediately after I sat down, I knew this was not going to help me either. I was so nauseous by then that I was sure the best thing for me to do would be to get out of the water and the boat. I looked over at Cindy and she seemed to be having the time of her life. She had already caught two fish, but I was too queasy to care. I felt as though I were going to throw up. I was so sorry I had gotten on the boat.

I started thinking about a few other people who had told me they had been seasick before, but it had never happened to me. Of course, I had never been deep sea fishing before either, and now I was making a promise to myself that I would never go again. Never, ever again!

I went inside the cabin and lay down on the sofa but I could still feel my stomach turning and churning. Everything was going every which way. First, the earth seemed to be upside down, then sideways, then up and down, and of course, all around. Everything was moving so fast. I could not even close my eyes to escape the terrible dizziness and sickness. *What am I going to do? I have to get off this boat!* I thought. *Where will I go? There is nowhere to go but in the deep, gigantic ocean, but I am certainly not feeling well enough to swim. I will drown if I jump in now,* I told myself.

I decided to go climb up the ladder to where Homer was. *Maybe he'll let me drive the boat and I'll feel better,* I thought to myself. I made it about halfway up when I looked back down at the water and thought I just might fall into the ocean. If I didn't fall, I decided that maybe I should just go ahead and jump in. I didn't know what to do. I was so confused. I felt sure, though, that the ladder was the wrong place for me to be. It seemed like no matter where I went or what I did, nowhere or nothing was right for me. Not one single thing made me feel any better. I told myself one thing, though. *If I ever get off this boat, I will never get back on another one. No one can pay me any amount of money to go deep sea fishing again. This event will surely be enough for me,* I thought.

In spite of it all, I was still tempted to just jump into the water to escape the seasickness. "Oh my God!" I prayed out loud to Jesus. I asked the Lord to help me. I had never felt this bad in my entire life. No matter what, the horrific feeling was not going anywhere but with me. I asked the guys if they would go back to shore because I thought I was going to die. They told me that they would start the boat up and drive to a new place. They said maybe this would help me. I was so thankful for anything they were willing to do to make things better for me. I was definitely at their mercy now.

Thank God, riding in the boat again with the wind blowing in my face made my seasickness subside. I was so relieved that I gave both guys a great big hug for moving the boat. A few minutes later, I started fishing, and guess what? I caught the largest Spanish mackerel the guys said they had ever seen before. I caught three or four more fish that day, while Cindy caught several, too. My first fish was the largest of them, though, the guys had told me. It was so huge that I decided to have a replica made of it. I wanted to take it home and hang it on my wall. After all, it was the first fish I had ever caught, and it was unusually large, so I had to have it for a souvenir. I also felt I deserved it after all the seasickness I had endured.

When I arrived home and after my replica had been sent to me via mail, I hung my monster fish on the wall. One day my daughter, Mindy, walked over and touched the fish with her hand. She was making weird faces at it, telling me that she couldn't believe I would stuff a fish and mount it on my wall. I laughed out loud when I told Mindy that it was just a replica and not the actual fish. Mindy actually looked relieved when I told her that we had already cleaned and eaten the real one.

Later that week, there was a story printed in the city's newspaper about a man who had caught the very same type fish that I had caught. In the article, the writer wrote about how large the Spanish mackerel was that he had caught, and how much it weighed. Yes, the writer had made a very big deal about it, when in fact my fish had weighed a few ounces more than his had.

Oh well, it doesn't really matter, I thought. *If someone had wanted to print a story about my huge fish, they'd probably have to write about my seasickness, too.* Needless to say, this was something I couldn't wait to forget. I had almost put it out of my mind the same way I had almost forgotten about my child birth pain after my babies had been born. Keep in mind that I said "almost," but not totally.

Deep down inside, I will never completely forget that dreadful day I spent on the boat out in the deep blue ocean. Again, I was sicker than I'd ever been in my entire life. Now, when it comes to deep sea fishing, I have only one thing to say about it. "Hopefully, no one will ever talk me into going for a second time because the last thing in the whole wide world I ever want to be again is **'sick for a fish.'"**

The Winner's Circle

A circle of friends and family,
Cannot be beaten, most definitely.

D.J. DeSai

I know money can buy a lot of things but I don't think it can buy the love that ties family and friends close together. This takes respect and honesty. Without these, I believe our love is molded in sand and will easily fall apart. I also think that spending time with the ones we love can build a bridge that will join our family together forever. Hold on to those memories, too. They mean everything. This one means so much to me that I desire to share it in this story.

One Friday night, my parents called me to ask me to go to the race track with them the next day. They owned a few race horses and one of them was scheduled to run in the ninth race, which was the feature race of the day. I told them I didn't think I could get off from work, especially since their horse was racing on a Saturday, and this was the busiest day of the week at my workplace. I thanked my parents for the invitation, but I told them I'd probably have to pass.

I went to work the next day, excited about my parents' horse running that afternoon, and wishing so badly that I could go to the track, too. Logically, I knew I shouldn't go because, financially, I couldn't afford to. I needed to work because I desperately needed money to pay some of my bills that I had gotten behind on. As a matter of fact, if I were to leave work early, I would not make any money at all because I was only paid a percentage of how much I earned, depending on the amount of business I had. I couldn't make money if I wasn't there, so the horse races were pretty much out of the question. I started feeling down in the dumps about not being able to spend time with my family that day.

Early that morning I walked over to a little store next to my workplace to buy a cup of coffee. The manager of the store, whose name was Ted, asked me if I thought my parents' horse would win that day. I proudly told him yes, not really knowing for sure if the horse had a chance or not. I was just trying to be positive while joking around with him at the same time. I really liked Ted. He was a nice guy.

Ted told me he liked another horse that was racing in the same race as my parents' horse. He also told me that this particular horse was a long shot, which meant the horse was not expected to win. He asked me if I was going to go to the track. I told him I didn't think I could go because I needed to work. He asked me if I wanted him to make a bet for me. I told him no at first, but when I realized I had two extra dollars in my pocket I handed the bills to Ted and told him yes. I told him I would love for him to get a ticket for me. I asked him if he would get me a two-dollar exacta bet on my parents' horse to come in first place along with the horse he liked to come in second place. This bet meant that those two horses would have to come in first and second, and in that exact order.

I thanked Ted for getting me an exacta ticket. He sure did love the horse races, so it was fun for me to give him money to bet on my parents' horse along with his favorite horse pick in the same race. *This is as good a bet as any,* I thought to myself, *and it will be fun to pick a couple of horses since I can't go to the track.*

When I handed Ted the two dollar bills, he looked at me with a startled look on his face and asked me if I wanted him to box the two horses. He said, "Dory, if you box both horses, it will cost you only two dollars more." He went on to remind me that betting an exacta box would give me more of a chance to win. Boxing the two horses would mean that either horse could come in either way instead of only the one way I had already told Ted to bet for me.

After thinking about Ted's betting idea for a moment, I was quick to say, "Nah, that's okay." I told him I felt confident that my parents' horse would win the race. "Maybe your horse will come in second place and I'll win some money," I laughed while joking around with him. I thanked Ted again for getting my ticket and then walked out of the store, still wishing that I could go to the races and join everyone else in all the fun.

Around lunch time, the business at my workplace had slowed down some and most of the employees, including myself, were just sitting around looking at each other. It was such a beautiful, sunshiny, autumn day outside, and I was becoming very fidgety. I finally decided to ask my boss if I could leave early. *I'm not making any money anyway, so why stay?* I asked myself. I told my boss that most of my family was meeting at the race track, and I would love to go visit with all of them. He told me to go ahead and go since the business had slacked off. I was so excited to get out of there!

Before I left, I hurriedly picked up the phone and called my Aunt Vera. I couldn't wait to ask her if she'd like to ride to the race track with me. My aunt was quick to say yes, with excitement in her voice. She told me she would start getting ready.

After I arrived home, I changed my clothes and then drove to Aunt Vera's house to pick her up. We headed to the race track, both of us talking and laughing while enjoying the beautiful day together. The leaves on the trees had turned into the most beautiful colors of orange, brown, red, and yellow. There was very little green left so the picture perfect scenery was simply amazing to see.

When the two of us arrived at the track, I realized I did not have any money with me except for one five dollar bill and one hundred dollar bill. My parents had given me the one hundred dollar bill for my birthday a couple of weeks prior. One of their thoroughbreds had won a previous race, so they had shared their winnings with me, giving me a special birthday gift. I had decided to save it for a rainy day. Although rain was the last thing in the big, blue sky, I decided it would be the perfect day to spend the money.

I found the one hundred dollar bill all wadded up, hidden in my wallet underneath a picture of my mom and dad. I told my Aunt Vera I wanted to go bet on my parents' horse before it was too late as I stuck the big bill inside my jeans pocket. This was the only race that I was going to bet on since we had arrived at the track so late. We had thirty minutes to spare before my parents' horse was scheduled to run in the feature race.

Feeling confident, I walked up to the betting window, took out my one hundred dollar bill, and told the teller I wanted a five-dollar exacta bet. I recited the number of my parents' horse to him which was the number one horse. Then I told him I wanted to put the number one horse on top to win with all the other horses to come in second place. This bet meant that my parents' horse had to win the race, but any other horse in the race could come in second place. This bet used up around fifty dollars of my one hundred dollar bill, leaving me half of the remaining money to get a win, place, and show ticket on the horse. This bet meant that I would win money if my parents' horse came in first, second, or third. The teller handed me several tickets, and I stuck them all inside my jeans pocket, and then walked off with Aunt Vera to find the rest of our family.

I had never bet this much money on one race before in my entire life. I still don't know what possessed me to do this. Maybe it was the beautiful day, or could it have been that I just felt lucky? Maybe it was because we had only gotten there for one race, so I felt as though I needed to make the trip worth my while. After all, I had taken off from work to go to the track, which was over an hour drive for just that one horse race. The thought had also crossed my mind for just one quick moment that maybe I should have saved the one hundred dollars for bills that would soon need to be paid, but I was feeling so spontaneous and secure. After all, the money was a birthday gift from my mom and dad, so I decided to spend it all on their race horse. Evidently, I was in the mood to gamble and take a chance. I quickly put my personal bills on the back burner in my mind. I would just have to buckle down with my money later.

When Aunt Vera and I found our family, they all greeted the two of us with hugs and kisses, telling us they were so glad we could make it. Aunt Vera and I were so happy too, just to be surrounded by our loved ones on such a beautiful day. It was like a family reunion and I was feeling so blessed. It did me good to get away from my job, although the guilty feelings kept haunting my mind about leaving work early, and possibly missing out on money that I could not really afford to lose. It was easy to make those thoughts go away though. I was with my family, and the race was about to begin. My parents' horse was getting ready to run. There was so much excitement in the air, and I was feeling it all.

The entire family hovered over the big screen television as we watched the horses break from the gate. Soon they all rounded the first turn. It was a long race, and the top winning jockey had taken off for the lead riding his horse. The leading horse was also the chosen favorite in the race, and was soon to be ten lengths ahead of all the other horses. Sad to say, my parents' horse was dead last. I kept my eyes glued to my parents' horse, which was a filly. I had watched the horse since the gates had first opened and the horses had taken off. I knew my parents' filly had a history of always breaking for last place in the beginning of every race. The horse needed a long race to have time to catch up with the other horses before their last turn for home. This particular race was a long race, so I had high hopes the filly would win.

Sure enough, I saw my parents' horse start to run harder. She was coming on fast. She was making her move and running as quickly as her legs would go. By the time the horse arrived at the last turn, I was certain she was going to win. Her ears were flopping in the wind as she passed all of the other horses. Yes, she was on a mission to make it to the finish line first. Since the race was so long, she had plenty of time to catch up with the others. By the time she had caught up, the other horses had started tiring out, along with the favorite chosen horse in the race. The filly was full of energy at the right time to win the race.

I turned to my dad and said, "There she goes, Daddy! There she goes." I told my dad that their horse was going to win the race but he said, "No, Dory, that's not her!" I said, "Yes, Daddy! Yes! That is her!" I knew it was my parents' filly in the lead because again, my eyes had not left the horse since the beginning of the race. My dad must have seen the filly's number flashing on the television screen, because he finally started getting excited, too. He started snapping his fingers and yelling, "Come on! Come on!" By this time, everyone was yelling for the horse. Yes, their filly won the race by three or four lengths. "Wow! What a beautiful day at the race track," I shouted.

Everyone ran outside to the winner's circle to have their picture made with the winning filly. I was so excited, along with everyone else. There were several family members and close friends proudly standing together. We all got our picture made with the winning horse in the winner's circle. It was a circle of love, too.

I was so glad that I had left work early that day. I couldn't have had any more fun than what I was having at that very moment. My mom and dad were so happy, too. Everyone stayed around and talked for a while longer, making plans to visit each other again soon, before we all said our goodbyes.

After everyone in the family had left the race track, Aunt Vera and I started walking toward the car. With a curious look on her face, Aunt Vera turned to me and asked me how much money I won. I told her I did not know, because I had forgotten all about my winning tickets inside my blue jeans pocket. I could not believe I was getting ready to leave the race track without cashing my winning tickets. I told Aunt Vera to wait for me in the car, and I would be right back.

Excitedly, I ran to the cashier's window, and laid my tickets down on the counter. The teller took them, ran them through the machine, and then counted back the mega bills to me. "Oh my God!" I shouted out to heaven.

"What a blessing! Thank you Jesus!" I screamed. I saw one hundred dollar bills, fifty dollar bills, twenty dollars bills, ten dollar bills, five dollar bills, and one dollar bills sitting in a pile on the counter. The stack of money was lying in front of me, and I could not believe my eyes. I did not even count the cash, nor did I know how much the cashier had counted back to me. I was in a state of shock! I had no idea I had won that much money, and still didn't know how much it really was. I thanked the teller while handing her a twenty dollar bill for a tip. Then I picked up all of the bills and crammed them inside my jeans pocket, as I headed back to the car where Aunt Vera was waiting for me.

As the two of us drove away, I shouted out, "I won!" "Oh! Great, Dory! How much money did you win?" Aunt Vera asked. "I won a lot," I said, as I pointed to the big bulge sticking out of my pants pocket. My aunt smiled at me. I told her that I had won plenty enough money for us to go out somewhere that night to celebrate. I also told her that we would both be wearing new dresses, compliments of my winnings. We laughed, sang songs, and celebrated as we drove the beautiful drive back home.

While driving on cloud nine, I was so glad that I had gone ahead and left work early that day. I could not have earned that much money working the entire week. I was also grateful for the money, which I needed so desperately to help pay my bills. Now I had it, plus much more. I silently thanked God, and then I told my Aunt Vera how appreciative I was, too.

After we arrived home, I did what I told my aunt I would do. We went shopping, and I bought each of us a beautiful dress to wear out that night. We got all made up, dressed up, and then headed out to our favorite place to listen to music and dance. We had a great time that night, still celebrating our family reunion and the big horse race win. Life was grand!

Feeling nothing but tired when we got back home that night, I couldn't wait to go to bed. The entire day and night had been so exciting, but yet so exhausting. However, I did not sleep well that night from thinking about what I would do with all the money I had won. I thanked God for my blessings again, and reminded myself to tithe more than usual in church the next day.

I rested around the house the next afternoon. I didn't do much except remember the sweet memories of the previous day. My thoughts were so comforting and relaxing. I didn't want to ever forget them, so I replayed them over and over in my mind as many times as I could that day.

Soon, it was bed time again. I had to get up early the next morning. I needed to run some errands, pay my bills, and clean the house. I decided to deposit most of my money into my checking account, so I wouldn't spend it. I had won more than sixteen hundred dollars, but I had spent at least one hundred dollars of it already. I didn't mind, though. It was worth every penny to me. For several months I had wanted to take Aunt Vera out on the town, because she had been going through such a rough time in her life. She had helped me out in the past too, so it made me feel good to do this for her. Besides, the two of us had a blast that night, so I did not have any regrets when it came to spending the money. We deserved it. We were both hard workers and we needed a break. I felt good about giving us both just one night out with no financial worries whatsoever. Aunt Vera was also very appreciative.

The next day, I had to go back to work. No, I had not won enough money to retire from my job, although it would have been nice. Honestly though, I have always enjoyed my job.

Early that morning, I walked over to the little store across the street from my workplace to get my coffee as usual. After I walked inside the store, I saw the owner, Ted, walking toward me. He was smiling from ear to ear, as he handed me a wad of money. I asked him what it was, and he told me it was the money I had won on the horse race. I stood there and looked at Ted with a blank, puzzled look on my face. I did not understand. Ted quickly reminded me of the race that he had bet for me the previous Saturday, and of the two dollars I had given him to do it with. "Oh my goodness!" I screamed. I thought I was going to fall over when I counted the money Ted had handed me. I was holding three one hundred dollar bills and one fifty dollar bill in the palm of my hand. I quickly told Ted that I could not accept that much money from him. I went on to explain to him that I had gone to the track later that day, after telling him I probably wouldn't be able to. I told him about the money I had won. Again, I told him to take the money back.

We stood there for a few more moments talking, while Ted kept refusing to take the money. He told me it was rightfully mine. I told him I would split it with him for getting the bet for me. He shook his head no, telling me that he had won money at the track that day, too. Ted also told me that he had won much more money than I had. I offered him one of the one hundred dollar bills he had handed me, but he declined that, too. Then I held up the fifty dollar bill, demanding that Ted take that much at least. Again, he told me no. He said he was so grateful to have won as much money as he had. I didn't know what to say. I was so surprised!

Ted went on to say, "Thank you, Dory, for giving me the tip on your parents' horse." I laughed and said, "You're so welcome," although I knew I had not given Ted a tip. I did not know for certain that my parents' horse would win the race. I was only teasing around with him when I told him it would win. Most people would call it luck, although I told Ted I was thanking the Lord for the money I had won. I believed it was a blessing from above, even coming from a horse race. I did not feel guilty for gambling either, because I knew I did not have a problem or an addiction to it. I felt sure that God could and would bless me in this kind of situation, so I wanted to give him all of the glory for it.

Again, Ted reminded me that he had won a lot more money than I had, and I was sure he had. I was so happy for him. I was also happy for myself. I couldn't believe that I had turned the one hundred dollar bill my parents had given me for my birthday into more than sixteen hundred dollars. I also couldn't believe I had turned the two dollars I had given to Ted into three-hundred fifty dollars. This was a lot of money to me.

After paying all my bills, there were two things that I really wanted to buy. I wanted a new microwave oven and a new color television for my bedroom. I went out the next day and bought them both. I knew if I didn't, I'd probably end up using all the money sooner or later for bills. Now, I have something else besides my wonderful memories to remind me of that beautiful, blessed, and profitable day I got to spend with most of my family inside **"the winner's circle."**

Water Logged

Although loved ones leave us, and we wonder why,
Their memories are cherished, and never die.

D.J. DeSai

Something I have learned over the years is that oftentimes an embarrassing or frightful event can eventually turn into a precious memory. Time is the healer for many things, but time can also be quick to put a closure on something or someone you love very much. This is why I try to convince myself to lighten up and feel the sunshine, even when I walk through a tragic storm. Life is too short, so hold on to it tightly, as I am holding on to this story.

Several years ago, I decided to drive to Florida for a week of vacation fun. I knew I would be taking my two children with me, and much to my surprise, my Aunt Irene asked if she could go, too. I screamed out, "Yes, the more the merrier!" I knew we would all have a great time together. She said, "Oh! Thank you, Dory! I can't wait to get away."

After we arrived in Florida, and after a couple of days of relaxation, I was ready to do something besides lie on the beach and soak up the sun. I told my aunt it might be fun for us to rent some rafts and float out on the waves while getting a sun tan at the same time. We could also keep cool by being in the water. Besides, I dearly loved the ocean.

Aunt Irene kept telling me to go ahead and go, assuring me that she would stay on the beach and watch, because she couldn't swim. Irene was more than terrified of the water. I knew all about her fear because I could remember my aunt saying she would never trust herself in water any deeper than what she would run in her own bathtub. She was very serious about that, too.

After much more of my begging and pleading, Irene finally agreed to rent a raft with us. My daughter, Mindy, and I had convinced Aunt Irene that we would not go out too far in the water, and that we would be absolutely safe. I was sure my six-year-old daughter had shamed Aunt Irene into going, because Mindy was one little girl who had no fear of water whatsoever. My son had been spending time on the beach with another boy his same age. He was being supervised by the little boy's parents, so I could keep both eyes on Mindy and Aunt Irene while we were out in the ocean.

During our first hour out on the rafts, we stayed in very shallow water. I wanted to pacify my aunt and to also watch my brave daughter closely. Yes, Mindy seemed to be having the time of her life, and she was so full of energy. Needless to say, Irene and I were growing very tired. Riding the waves consisted of walking against the current, out into the water, climbing up on our rafts, and then riding them back to shore. There was too much physical work involved, and our ride back wasn't lasting long enough for us to rest.

Needless to say, it didn't take the three of us very long to start going a little further out into the ocean. We all agreed that we could ride our rafts back to shore for a longer amount of time if we went further out. We wanted to relax, especially us two older women. Also, Irene seemed to be getting much braver in the water as the day went by, so she didn't mind going a little further out. I was happy that she was finally having such a good time in the ocean. After all, Irene loved Florida so much, and all she ever really wanted to do was lie in the sun and watch people. *Who knows?* I asked myself. *Maybe Aunt Irene will even learn how to swim while we're here.*

Later that afternoon, the waves started getting much higher as the water became a lot rougher. *Wow! The wind is really picking up so there must be a storm coming in*, I thought. It had also started getting harder for us to climb up on our rafts. The waves kept trying to knock us off after we had gotten on. I would help Aunt Irene get on her raft, and then Mindy and I would help each other get up on ours. We would hold on to each other while trying to balance each other's rafts. It wasn't an easy thing to do, as the waves kept pounding us harder.

The last time the three of us got ready to float back to shore I noticed we were pretty far out. I couldn't believe how high and how fast the waves were coming in. The three of us were screaming and laughing, having so much fun riding and fighting the waves. Soon, I found myself getting a little worried about the water movement. It was getting rougher by the minute. I knew it was time for us to get out of the ocean, and I yelled at Mindy and Aunt Irene and told them so.

Suddenly, the direction of the waves seemed to change, as the wind blew harder. We all started floating back to shore going sideways instead of straight back. It seemed as though we were going further and further out into the ocean too, instead of back in toward shore. *Gee! We're moving so fast out here! It's hard for me to tell which way we're all going.* I thought. It was almost impossible for us to stay on our rafts. We were holding on as tightly as we could. I was worried about Mindy and Irene, because I couldn't see them part of the time because the waves were so high. I also thought I could see worried looks on their faces when I did catch a glimpse of them. I didn't want to alarm them any more than they already were, but the waves had gotten so high and the water was separating all of us for the first time that day. *This will definitely be our last lap on the rafts,* I thought to myself. I knew it was much too dangerous out there. I was more than worried, but I couldn't let it be known. I didn't want to make matters worse by causing my daughter and my aunt to panic.

When I finally started floating back toward the beach area, I looked up and saw my daughter Mindy. "Oh my God!" I shouted out to the Lord. Mindy was headed straight toward some logs that were standing in the water attached to the boardwalk. She was traveling so fast as she rode the hard waves. I started praying. I became very frightened, scared that my daughter's float would crash into one of the wooden logs. I was so worried that Mindy might get hurt. I started screaming and yelling as loudly as I could. I was trying to get my daughter's attention to tell her to try and slow down and to watch out for the logs. It was a hard task for me to try and guide my own raft in the same direction as my daughter's was headed, because the waves were taking us where they wanted to take us. Thank God, my raft started moving in the same direction as Mindy's was, although my raft wasn't floating as fast as Mindy's seemed to be. I tried to hurry and get closer to her to make sure she was safe until we both finally arrived at the boardwalk about the same time.

"Praise God!" I whispered. "Mindy is safe." Yes, I knew everything was okay by then, because we had both passed the big logs at the same time. I could also see the bottom of the ocean by then. Surprisingly, the water was only knee deep when Mindy and I got off our rafts just past the boardwalk. I was relieved, because it looked much deeper while we were still lying on the rafts. I assumed it was deeper anyway, probably because we were being pushed so hard by the deadly waves. I told Mindy not to go back out into the water anymore because the current had gotten so bad. She told me that she did not want to go back out because the ocean had really scared her. I smiled as I hugged my daughter.

All of a sudden I heard the most frantic voice coming from behind me. As I listened to the enormous screams, I was sure everyone near the boardwalk had heard them, too. The horrific yelling did not let up. I quickly turned around to see Aunt Irene. "Oh my goodness!" I gasped. My aunt was lying face down on her raft with an outrageously frightened look on her face, screaming as loudly as she could. *Oh no!* I thought to myself. I had completely forgotten all about her while worrying so much about Mindy's safety. Aunt Irene was holding on for dear life to one of the wooden logs that I had tried to keep my daughter from running into. Irene kept crying and screaming, "Help me! Help me! Please! Somebody help me!" over and over again.

Feeling somewhat embarrassed, I yelled at my aunt several times, trying to let her know that I was on my way to where she was, but she wouldn't stop yelping long enough to listen to me. She couldn't hear me because of the noise coming out of her own mouth. *Gee! I know exactly why Aunt Irene is screaming*, I thought. *She thinks the water is over her head, especially after she heard me yelling at Mindy, trying to get her to slow her raft down so she wouldn't run into the wooden logs attached to the boardwalk.*

Again, I yelled at Aunt Irene, trying my best to assure her the water was not deep where she was. I tried to get closer to her so she could hear what I was saying, but she was still screaming so loudly that she couldn't hear anything. As Irene continued to hold on tightly to the wooden log, all anyone could hear was "Help me! Help me! I can't swim!" I knew I shouldn't laugh at my aunt because I could tell she was terrified, but I couldn't help myself. Aunt Irene was still thinking the water was over her head, but it wasn't. Yes, she was thinking she was in great danger because, again, she was more than scared of the water. If she would only be quiet for a second, I could tell her the water was only knee deep, but this certainly was not happening.

Thank God, I finally made it over to where she was. I told my aunt to get off the raft, but she continued to scream bloody murder. She was having a panic attack, and she could not hear anything I was saying to her. She would not let go of the log. The rough waves had scared her to death. She must have been in shock while lying face down on her raft and drenched by the water. Irene was still thinking she needed to be rescued. She was still afraid she was going to drown.

I quickly walked directly in front of my aunt to visually show her where the water level was. I pointed to my knees, proving to her that she was not in water over her head. Finally, I saw a look of relief on her face, as the lifeguards kept blowing their whistles from the boardwalk. They kept motioning for us to get out of the water and for Aunt Irene to let go of the log. There must have been over one hundred folks looking at us from the top of the boardwalk by then. There was certainly more people than that on the beach watching us, wondering what in the world was wrong with Aunt Irene. I was sure that each one of them thought she was hurt or had been bitten by a shark. Her continuous screaming for help had alarmed everyone. Not one person, though, thought she was drowning, because everyone else knew that was not possible. They could see her on the raft, and they knew the water was shallow where she was.

When Aunt Irene finally got up from her raft, everyone started clapping. I could tell she was so embarrassed when she realized the water was only knee deep. Her screams had caused so many people to look at her. Yes, she had become the center of attention. When my aunt turned around to face me and all the other people that were watching from the beach and boardwalk area, I was sure I had never been more embarrassed for anyone in my entire life.

"Oh my goodness!" I screamed. Aunt Irene's bathing suit top had come all the way undone and her breasts were hanging out all over the place. I was sure the hook to her top had come loose from the hard knocks of the waves, and her struggle to hang on to the log. I yelled at Aunt Irene, telling her to tie her top. *Gee! Golly!* I thought. She was just innocently standing there putting on a show.

Finally, when my aunt realized her top was only hanging on to her body by one hook, she looked as though she had seen a ghost. She looked down and saw everything she had hanging out as visible as the Florida sunshine. Everyone else was still watching, too. Irene's face dropped, and I knew without a doubt that she would have hidden underneath the water if she hadn't been so terrified of it. Instead, she ran behind the log to try and get her bathing suit together again. After she had finished, everyone started clapping again. "What a day at sea!" I mumbled under my breath. Aunt Irene had nothing but a red face as she received the ovation.

Needless to say, I was sure my aunt was more afraid of the water now than she ever was. That didn't stop both of us from laughing about it, though. I will never forget the way she had hung on to that log thinking she was going to drown. Although she will probably never go back out into the water again, she and I have agreed on one thing. Our ocean episode will go down in our family history book as being the one time in Aunt Irene's life that she and I can honestly and truly describe her as being **"water logged."**

Several years later, Aunt Irene told me and the entire family that she had been diagnosed with terminal cancer. She was fifty-eight years old. My aunt had gone to the doctor because she was feeling weak. The doctor did some blood work, and then admitted her to the hospital for some more tests. He determined a couple of days later that her cancer was in stage four. He gave her less than one year to live. Aunt Irene spent a couple of weeks in the hospital, and went straight from there to a nursing home. This is where I visited her today, as we talked and laughed about our adventure on our rafts in the ocean.

I realize I may not have my Aunt Irene with me much longer than only a few short months, but the sweet memory we shared will last a lifetime. I thank God every day for my story I call **"Water Logged."**

Nine months after Aunt Irene was diagnosed with cancer, she passed away. I've dedicated this short story to her, and I believe with all my heart that she is still laughing about it with me. Irene was like the sister I never had, and I miss her immensely. I will always hold this story close to my heart. Now, I feel at peace and blessed just knowing that my dear aunt is safe in the arms of our Lord Jesus Christ, and she will never be afraid of water again.

Mom's Best Interest

Moms are angels who watch over you,
They have your back in all that you do.

D.J. DeSai

Moms are amazing. They nurture us from the time we are born until the very end. Thankfully, I still have my sweet mother with me, and I believe there is not another one in the entire world who could ever measure up to her. I love my mom with all my heart so, naturally, this "Dory Story" is dedicated to her.

Some time ago, I had been allowing some of my friends and clients to read a few of my short stories that I'd previously written. I had decided to get some input from others before going through the process of having my book published. I only wanted to find out if anyone had a special interest in my writing, and I wondered if my book was even worth the time and expense to go the extra mile. Thankfully, almost every response I received was positive and encouraging, especially one from a male friend of mine named Allen.

One day Allen stopped by my business. He asked me if I would let him read a few more of my short stories. He had only read one story so far, and he told me he really enjoyed reading it. I was flattered that Allen was so complimentary concerning my writing, so I told him, yes. Of course, I wanted him to read a couple more of my stories, hoping he would continue to critique my writing. This was very important to me. Before Allen left the business, he and I set up a time and place to meet that same night.

At a nearby restaurant around seven o'clock, I sat with Allen while he read three or four more of my stories. He was quick to tell me that he loved all that he had read thus far. I thanked him but told him I was running out of time and needed to go home. I picked up my book and told my friend I'd see him later. Surprisingly, Allen began pleading with me, asking for my permission to take my book home with him so he could read all of it. I told him no, because I only had one copy of each story printed on paper. Allen seemed disappointed. He asked me if I would print him out a copy of my entire book the next day. I told him I would think about it, but I really wanted to tweak my book a little more before allowing any one person to read all of it.

Although I felt very touched that Allen was so interested in my book, I wondered if it were a good idea to allow him to read all of it. I wasn't sure I was ready for that much of my writing to be exposed to one person. I still felt somewhat insecure concerning my artistry. On the other hand, though, I thought that maybe it was a good idea.

Still feeling a little leery and confused about Allen's proposal, I decided to call my mother that night to talk to her on the phone about it. When she answered, I didn't waste any time telling her about my meeting with Allen and all that he had said about my book. I felt very proud to tell my mom that someone had loved my short stories that much.

Surprisingly, there was a brief silence on the other end of the phone before my dear mother fearfully spoke up and said, "Oh no, Dory! You'd better not let him take your entire book home with him." She was quick to tell me that she did not think it was a good idea at all for me to agree to let Allen read all of it. I was sure I knew exactly what my mom must be insinuating and thinking. I quickly assured my mother that Allen was a good friend of mine, and that he surely was not trying to steal my book if that was what she was so concerned about. I went on to explain to her that he did not have any other motive in mind but to read my book. As I laughed out loud, I teasingly told my mom, "Allen is not a book thief, Mother! He's my friend!"

Holding the telephone close to my ear, I laughed even harder when I heard my sweet mom say, "No, Dory! That is not what I meant! I'm not worried about your friend stealing your book, but I most certainly do not think you should let him read all of it. If he reads it all, he won't want to buy one!"

"Oh my God," I whispered to Jesus. Suddenly, I had a strong desire to look up to heaven and thank the Lord for my dear mother. What a blessing!

I knew her sweet words were more than genuine. Feeling nothing but joy deep down in my heart for all of my mom's wisdom and concern, I was certain she had my back. Yes, if there was ever anything in this whole wide world that I would surely never want to live without, it would have to be my **"mom's best interest."**